CODE SWIFTLY

UNLOCK THE POWER OF APPLE'S PROGRAMMING LANGUAGE

HAWKINGS J CROWD

Preface

Welcome to the exciting world of Swift programming! Whether you're a complete beginner eager to learn your first coding language or an experienced developer looking to expand your skills, this book is designed to be your comprehensive guide to mastering Swift.

In today's rapidly evolving tech landscape, Swift stands out as a powerful, intuitive, and modern programming language. Created by Apple, it empowers developers to build exceptional applications for iOS, macOS, watchOS, tvOS, and beyond. Swift's clean syntax, robust features, and strong community support make it an ideal choice for anyone passionate about creating innovative software.

This book aims to take you on a structured journey through the fundamentals and advanced concepts of Swift. We'll start with the basics, ensuring you grasp the core principles, and gradually progress to more complex topics like concurrency, architecture, and UI development with SwiftUI. You'll find a blend of clear explanations, practical examples, and hands-on exercises to reinforce your learning and build your confidence.

What You'll Find Inside:

Comprehensive Coverage: From variables and data types to protocols and generics, we'll cover all the essential aspects of Swift programming.

Practical Examples: Each chapter includes real-world code examples to illustrate key concepts and demonstrate how to apply them in your projects.

Hands-On Exercises: Reinforce your learning with practical exercises that challenge you to apply what you've learned.

Modern Swift Techniques: Explore the latest features of Swift, including `async/await`, actors, and SwiftUI, to build cutting-edge applications.

Best Practices: Learn industry-standard best practices for writing clean, efficient, and maintainable Swift code.

App Architecture and Deployment: Gain insights into project setup, app architecture, and how to deploy your apps to the simulator and physical devices.

Who This Book Is For:

Beginners with no prior programming experience.

Developers transitioning from other programming languages.

Anyone interested in building iOS, macOS, watchOS, or tvOS applicationsStudents and educators looking for a comprehensive Swift learning resource.

Why Swift?

Swift's elegance and efficiency make it a pleasure to work with. Its safety features help prevent common programming errors, and its performance rivals that of traditional languages like C++. With Swift, you'll be able to bring your creative ideas to life and build apps that delight users.

Happy coding!

TABLE OF CONTENTS

Chapter 7

Chapter 8

Chapter 9

Chapter 10

10.1 Project Setup and App Architecture

10.2 Connecting UI Elements to Code

10.3 Deploying Your App to the Simulator/Device

Chapter 1

Getting Started with Swift

1.1 Setting Up Your Development Environment

Introduction:

Vivid Explanation

Imagine building a house without a solid foundation. It's unstable, prone to problems, and likely to collapse. Similarly, attempting to learn Swift without a properly configured development environment is a recipe for frustration. A well-set-up environment provides the tools, structure, and stability needed for a smooth learning curve.

Xcode, Apple's powerful IDE, is the cornerstone of iOS, macOS, watchOS, and tvOS development. It's where you'll write, debug, and test your Swift code. Think of it as your digital workshop, equipped with everything you need to bring your app ideas to life

This section will gently guide you through the process of installing Xcode and familiarizing yourself with its essential components.

1.1.1 Installing Xcode:

Downloading Xcode:

Vivid Explanation:

The journey begins at the Mac App Store. Navigate to the App Store application on your Mac, and search for "Xcode." The download is substantial, so ensure you have a robust internet connection. Picture downloading a large, comprehensive toolkit; patience is key.

Apple sometimes releases beta versions of Xcode on their developer website, those are only for those with a developer account.

Installing Xcode:

Vivid Explanation:

Once the download completes, the installation process is largely automatic. Simply follow the on-screen prompts, agreeing to the license agreement. Xcode will install itself into your Applications folder, becoming a permanent fixture in your development arsenal.

Verifying the Installation:

Vivid Explanation:

To ensure everything went smoothly, launch Xcode. You should be greeted with the Xcode welcome screen. This confirms that your environment is ready for action.

Code (Not directly code, but a visual verification):

Look for the Xcode icon in your Applications folder and launch it. Observe the welcome window with options like "Create a new Xcode project" and "Check out an existing project."

1.1.2 Understanding Xcode Components:

Xcode Interface Overview:

Vivid Explanation

Xcode's interface is designed to streamline your workflow. The navigation area on the left provides access to your project files, symbols, and breakpoints. The editor area in the center is where you'll write and edit your Swift code. The utility area on the right offers inspectors and libraries for various tasks.

Imagine a well-organized workspace with distinct sections for different tools and materials.

Playgrounds:

Vivid Explanation:

Xcode Playgrounds are interactive environments where you can experiment with Swift code in real-time. They're perfect for learning new concepts, testing code snippets, and visualizing results. Think of them as a sandbox for your Swift experiments.

Code (Playground Example):

Swift
```
  // Open Xcode, go to File > New > Playground
  // Select a blank playground

  var greeting = "Hello, Playground!"
  print(greeting)

  let number = 10
  let squared = number * number
  print(squared)
```

As you type in a playground, the results are displayed immediately in the right sidebar.

Simulators:

Vivid Explanation:

Simulators are virtual devices that allow you to test your apps without needing physical hardware. You can choose from various iPhone, iPad, Apple Watch, and Apple TV models, each with different screen sizes and operating system versions.

Think of them as virtual testing grounds, allowing you to run your applications on many different virtual devices

To access simulators, in Xcode, in the top bar where the play button is, you can select which simulator to use.

1.1.3 Optional Setup and Considerations:
Apple Developer Account (Optional):
Vivid Explanation:
While not strictly necessary for learning Swift or using simulators, an Apple Developer account unlocks access to advanced features, such as deploying apps to physical devices and distributing them on the App Store. It's the key to taking your app development to the next level.

Apple's developer website is developer.apple.com
Xcode Preferences:
Vivid Explanation:
Xcode's preferences allow you to customize your development environment to your liking. You can change themes, code formatting, keyboard shortcuts, and more. Tailoring your preferences can significantly enhance your productivity.

Keeping Xcode Updated:
Vivid Explanation:
Apple regularly releases updates to Xcode, incorporating new features, bug fixes, and performance improvements. Staying up-to-date ensures you have access to the latest tools and technologies.

Xcode updates are available through the mac app store.

By providing these vivid explanations and code examples, you can create a truly engaging and informative section for your Swift programming book.

1.2 Understanding Swift Syntax Basics

Introduction:

Swift's syntax is designed for readability and clarity, making it easier for developers to write and understand code. It draws inspiration from various languages, aiming for a modern and intuitive approach. This section will introduce you to the fundamental elements of Swift syntax, providing a solid foundation for your coding journey.

1.2.1 Variables and Constants:

Vivid Explanation:

Variables and constants are the building blocks of data storage in Swift. Variables, declared with the `var` keyword, can have their values changed throughout the program. Constants, declared with `let`, hold values that remain fixed. This distinction promotes code safety and clarity.

Swift uses type inference, meaning it can often deduce the data type of a variable or constant based on its initial value. However, you can also explicitly specify the type.

Code Example:

```swift
Swift
  // Variable declaration
  var myAge = 30
  myAge = 31 // Changing the variable's value

  // Constant declaration
  let pi = 3.14159
```

// pi = 3.15 // This would cause an error, as constants cannot be changed

let myName: String = "Alice" //Explicit type declaration.

1.2.2 Data Types:
Vivid Explanation:

Swift is a type-safe language, meaning it enforces strict rules about data types. Common data types include `Int` (integers), `Double` (floating-point numbers), `String` (text), and `Bool` (Boolean values). Understanding these types is crucial for writing correct and efficient code.

Swift also uses Optionals, for when a variable may not have a value.

Code Example:

```Swift
let integerNumber: Int = 10
let decimalNumber: Double = 3.14
let text: String = "Hello, Swift!"
let isTrue: Bool = true
var optionalString: String? //This is an optional string.
optionalString = "This string now has a value"
```

1.2.3 Comments and Semicolons:
Vivid Explanation:

Comments are essential for documenting your code and making it more understandable. Swift supports single-line comments (using `//`) and multi-line comments (using `/* ... */`).

Unlike some other languages, Swift does not require semicolons at the end of each line. However, they can be used to separate multiple statements on a single line.

Code Example:

Swift

```
// This is a single-line comment
/*
  This is a multi-line comment.
  It can span multiple lines.
*/


  let x = 10; let y = 20 // Semicolons to separate multiple
statements
```

1.2.4 Printing to the Console:
Vivid Explanation:

The `print()` function is used to display output in the console, which is invaluable for debugging and understanding your code's behavior. It allows you to inspect the values of variables and constants during runtime.

Code Example:

Swift

```
let message = "Welcome to Swift!"
print(message) // Prints "Welcome to Swift!" to the console
print("The value of x is: \(x)") //String interpolation.
```

By breaking down Swift's syntax into these fundamental elements, you'll provide readers with a clear and comprehensive understanding of how to write basic Swift code.

1.3 Your First Swift Program: "Hello, World!"

Introduction:

Vivid Explanation:

The "Hello, World!" program is a time-honored tradition in programming, serving as a gentle introduction to a new language. It's a simple yet powerful way to verify that your development environment is set up correctly and to get a taste of Swift's syntax. In this section, we'll walk you through creating and running your first Swift program, demystifying the process and building your confidence.

We will be using Xcode Playgrounds for this, as it is the easiest way to begin writing swift code.

1.3.1 Creating a New Playground:

Vivid Explanation:

Xcode Playgrounds are interactive environments that allow you to write and execute Swift code in real-time. We'll start by creating a new Playground to house our "Hello, World!" program.

Open Xcode. Navigate to "File" -> "New" -> "Playground..."

Select a "Blank" playground and choose a location to save it.

Name your playground something like "HelloWorld"

Visual Aid:

Include a screenshot of the Xcode "New Playground" dialog box, highlighting the steps.

1.3.2 Writing the "Hello, World!" Code:

Vivid Explanation:

Inside your newly created Playground, you'll see a basic structure. We'll replace the default code with our "Hello, World!" program.

Swift's `print()` function is used to display output in the console. We'll use it to print the message "Hello, World!".

Code Example:

Swift

```
print("Hello, World!")
```

* **Explanation of the Code:**
    * `print()`: This is a function that displays the specified value in the console.
    * `"Hello, World!"`: This is a string literal, which is the message we want to display.

1.3.3 Running the Program and Viewing the Output:
Vivid Explanation:
In a Playground, the code executes automatically as you type. You'll see the output in the right-hand sidebar of the Playground window.

Observe the right sidebar of the playground. You should see "Hello, World!" displayed.

If you do not see it, ensure that the playground is not paused.

Visual Aid:
Include a screenshot of the Playground window with the "Hello, World!" output displayed in the sidebar.

1.3.4 Expanding on the Program:
Vivid Explanation:

Let's modify the program slightly to show that we can use variables inside of our print statement.

We will create a variable that will hold the hello world string, and then print that variable

Code Example:

Swift
```
let message = "Hello, World!"
print(message)
```

* **Explanation of the Code:**
    * We created a constant called message, and assigned the string "Hello, World!" to it.
    * We then printed the constant message.
    * This will produce the same output as the prior example.

1.3.5 Next steps:
Vivid Explanation:

Congratulate the reader on writing their first swift program.

Tell them that they have now taken their first step into the world of swift development.

Briefly explain what the next chapter will contain.

By following this structure, you'll provide readers with a clear, concise, and engaging introduction to writing and running their first Swift program.

Chapter 2

Variables, Constants, and Data Types

2.1 Declaring Variables and Constants

2.1 Declaring Variables and Constants

Introduction:

Vivid Explanation:

Imagine variables and constants as containers for storing information in your program. Variables are like containers with labels that you can change, while constants are like containers with labels that are permanently fixed. Understanding when to use each is crucial for writing safe and efficient Swift code.

This section will explain how to declare variables and constants, the differences between them, and best practices for their usage.

2.1.1 Variable Declaration (`var`)

Vivid Explanation:

Variables are declared using the `var` keyword. They are used when the value of a piece of data may change during the execution of your program.

Think of a variable as a storage location that can be updated as needed. For example, a player's score in a game would be stored in a variable because it changes throughout the game.

Code Examples:

Swift
```
  // Declaring a variable of type Int
  var currentScore = 0
  currentScore = 10 // Updating the variable's value
  print(currentScore) // Output: 10

  // Declaring a variable of type String
  var playerName = "New Player"
  playerName = "Updated Player Name"
  print(playerName) // Output: Updated Player Name

  //Declaring a variable with explicit type declaration.
  var age: Int = 25
  age = 30
  print(age) //Output: 30
```

* **Explanation of the Code:**
   * The `var` keyword indicates that we are declaring a variable.
    * We assign an initial value to the variable using the assignment operator (`=`).
   * We can change the value of a variable at any time.

2.1.2 Constant Declaration (`let`)
Vivid Explanation:

Constants are declared using the `let` keyword. They are used when the value of a piece of data should remain unchanged throughout the program.

Think of a constant as a storage location that is set once and then cannot be modified. For example, the value of pi or the number of days in a week would be stored in constants.

Code Examples:
Swift

```
// Declaring a constant of type Double
let pi = 3.14159
// pi = 3.15 // This would cause a compile-time error

// Declaring a constant of type String
let appName = "My Swift App"
// appName = "Another Name" // This would also cause an error

//Declaring a constant with explicit type declaration.
let maximumNumberOfLoginAttempts: Int = 10
```

* **Explanation of the Code:**
   * The `let` keyword indicates that we are declaring a constant.
      * We assign an initial value to the constant using the assignment operator (`=`).
   * Once a constant is assigned a value, it cannot be changed. Any attempt to change it will result in a compile-time error.

2.1.3 Type Inference vs. Explicit Type Annotation

Vivid Explanation:
Swift's type inference allows the compiler to automatically determine the data type of a variable or constant based on its initial value. This makes[1] the code more concise.

However, you can also explicitly specify the data type using type annotation, which can improve code clarity and prevent potential errors

Type inference is great for when the type is obvious. Explicit type annotation is great for when the type might be ambiguous, or for when you want to enforce a specific type.

Code Examples:

Swift

```swift
// Type inference
let inferredInteger = 10 // Swift infers Int
let inferredDouble = 3.14 // Swift infers Double
let inferredString = "Hello" // Swift infers String

// Explicit type annotation
let explicitInteger: Int = 10
let explicitDouble: Double = 3.14
let explicitString: String = "Hello"
```

2.1.4 Best Practices:

Vivid Explanation:

Use constants (`let`) whenever possible to promote code safety and prevent accidental modification of values.

Use variables (`var`) only when the value of a piece of data needs to change.

Consider using explicit type annotation when the type is not immediately obvious or when you want to enforce a specific type.

Choose descriptive names for your variables and constants to improve code readability.

By covering these aspects, you'll provide your readers with a comprehensive understanding of how to declare and use variables and constants in Swift.

2.2 Exploring Fundamental Data Types (Int, Double, String, Bool)

Introduction:

Vivid Explanation:

Data types are the classifications of data that determine the possible values for that data, the operations that can be performed on that data, and the way that data is stored in memory. Swift is a type-safe language, meaning it enforces strict rules about data types. Understanding these fundamental types is essential for building robust and reliable applications.

We will cover the four most common and basic data types that you will use in almost every Swift program.

2.2.1 Integers (`Int`)

Vivid Explanation:

Integers represent whole numbers without fractional components, such as -10, 0, and 42. Swift provides various integer types, including `Int`, `Int8`, `Int16`, `Int32`, and `Int64`, each with different storage sizes and ranges. The `Int` type is the most commonly used and automatically selects an appropriate size based on the platform.

Think of integers as counting numbers that can be positive, negative, or zero.

Code Examples:

Swift

```
let wholeNumber: Int = 10
let negativeNumber: Int = -5
let largeNumber: Int = 1000000

print("Whole Number: \(wholeNumber)")
print("Negative Number: \(negativeNumber)")
print("Large Number: \(largeNumber)")

let maxIntValue = Int.max
let minIntValue = Int.min

print("Max Int Value: \(maxIntValue)")
print("Min Int Value: \(minIntValue)")
```

* **Explanation of the Code:**
    * We declare integer constants using the `Int` type.
    * We can represent positive, negative, and large integer values.
    * `Int.max` and `Int.min` provide the maximum and minimum values that an `Int` can hold on the current platform.

2.2.2 Floating-Point Numbers (Double)
Vivid Explanation:

Floating-point numbers represent numbers with fractional components, such as 3.14, -0.5, and 2.0. Swift provides two floating-point types: Float and Double. Double represents a 64-bit floating-point number, offering greater precision than Float, which is a 32-bit floating-point number. Double is generally preferred for most applications.

Think of floating-point numbers as numbers that can have decimal points.

Code Examples:

Swift
```
let piValue: Double = 3.14159
let decimalNumber: Double = -0.75
let largeDecimal: Double = 1.23456789

print("Pi Value: \(piValue)")
print("Decimal Number: \(decimalNumber)")
print("Large Decimal: \(largeDecimal)")
```

* **Explanation of the Code:**
    * We declare floating-point constants using the `Double` type.
    * We can represent positive, negative, and large decimal values

2.2.3 Strings (`String`)
Vivid Explanation:

Strings represent sequences of characters, such as "Hello, World!", "Swift", and "123". Swift's `String` type is powerful and versatile, supporting Unicode characters and various string operations.

Think of strings as text or sequences of characters.

Code Examples:

Swift
```
let greeting: String = "Hello, Swift!"
let name: String = "Alice"
let emptyString: String = ""
```

```
print("Greeting: \(greeting)")
print("Name: \(name)")
print("Empty String: \(emptyString)")

let combinedString = greeting + " My name is " + name;

print("Combined String: \(combinedString)")
```

* **Explanation of the Code:**
    * We declare string constants using the `String` type.
    * We can represent text, names, and empty strings.
    * Strings can be combined using the `+` operator

2.2.4 Booleans (`Bool`)
Vivid Explanation:

Booleans represent logical values, either `true` or `false`. They are used for decision-making and conditional logic in your programs.

Think of booleans as switches that can be either on (true) or off (false).

Code Examples:

Swift
```
let isTrue: Bool = true
let isFalse: Bool = false

print("Is True: \(isTrue)")
print("Is False: \(isFalse)")

let result = 10 > 5
print("Result of 10 > 5: \(result)")
```

Explanation of the Code
We declare boolean constants using the `Bool` type.

We can represent `true` and `false` values.

Boolean values are often the result of logical comparisons.

2.3 Type Inference and Type Safety in Swift

Excellent choice! "Type Inference and Type Safety in Swift" are core concepts that distinguish Swift as a modern and robust language. Let's break them down thoroughly.

2.3 Type Inference and Type Safety in Swift

Introduction:

Vivid Explanation:

Swift's type system is designed to prevent errors and ensure code reliability. Two key features that contribute to this are type inference and type safety. Type inference allows the compiler to automatically deduce the data type of a variable or constant, while type safety prevents you from accidentally using data in a way that is incompatible with its type. Together, they make Swift code more concise and less prone to errors.

These concepts are essential to understand to write clean and effective code.

2.3.1 Type Inference:

Vivid Explanation:

Type inference is a feature that allows the Swift compiler to automatically determine the data type of a variable or constant based on its initial value. This eliminates the need for explicit type annotations in many cases, making your code more concise and readable.

The compiler analyzes the value you assign to a variable or constant and infers the appropriate type. For example, if you assign an integer value, the compiler infers the `Int` type.

Code Examples:

Swift

```swift
// Type inference examples
let age = 30 // Compiler infers Int
let price = 19.99 // Compiler infers Double
let message = "Hello, Swift!" // Compiler infers String
let isActive = true // Compiler infers Bool

print("Age: \(type(of: age))")
print("Price: \(type(of: price))")
print("Message: \(type(of: message))")
print("Is Active: \(type(of: isActive))")
```

Explanation of the Code:

In each example, we declare a constant without explicitly specifying its type.

The compiler automatically infers the appropriate type based on the assigned value.
`type(of:)` is used to print the type of the variable.
Benefits of Type Inference
Reduces code verbosity.
Improves code readability.
Allows for faster development

2.3.2 Type Safety:
Vivid Explanation:

Type safety is a feature that prevents you from accidentally using data in a way that is incompatible with its type. Swift enforces strict rules about data types, ensuring that you can only perform operations that are valid for a given type.

If you try to perform an invalid operation, such as adding a string to an integer, the compiler will generate an error. This helps to catch errors early in the development process.

Code Examples:

```Swift
  let number = 10
  let text = "Hello"

    // let result = number + text // This would cause a compile-time
error
  let stringNumber = String(number)
  let combinedString = stringNumber + text;
  print(combinedString)
```

Explanation of the Code:

The commented-out line would cause a compile-time error because you cannot directly add an integer and a string.

We can convert the integer to a string, and then add the two strings together.

Swift's type safety prevents accidental type mismatches, reducing the likelihood of runtime errors.

Benefits of Type Safety:

Prevents runtime errors.

Improves code reliability.

Makes code easier to maintain.

2.3.3 When to Use Explicit Type Annotations:

Vivid Explanation:

While type inference is a powerful feature, there are situations where explicit type annotations are necessary or beneficial.

When the compiler cannot infer the type, when you want to make the type more obvious, or when dealing with optionals, explicit type annotations are used
Code Examples:

Swift
```
// Explicit type annotation examples
let explicitAge: Int = 30
let explicitPrice: Double = 19.99
let explicitMessage: String = "Hello, Swift!"
let explicitIsActive: Bool = true

 var optionalName: String? = nil // Explicitly declaring an optional String
```

Explanation of the Code:
In these examples, we explicitly specify the data type using type annotations.

When using optionals, it is necessary to declare the type.

2.3.4 Combining Type Inference and Type Safety:

Vivid Explanation:
Swift's type inference and type safety work together to provide a powerful and flexible type system.

Type inference reduces code verbosity, while type safety prevents errors.

This results in cleaner, more reliable, and easier to maintain code.

By providing these detailed explanations and code examples, you'll give your readers a solid understanding of type inference and type safety in Swift.

Chapter 3

Control Flow and Logic

3.1 Conditional Statements: If, Else, and Switch

Introduction:

Vivid Explanation:

Conditional statements are the decision-making tools of programming. They allow your code to execute different blocks of code based on whether certain conditions are true or false. Swift provides three primary conditional statements: `if`, `else`, and `switch`. These statements enable your programs to respond dynamically to different inputs and situations.

This section will explain how to use these statements effectively to create flexible and responsive Swift code.

3.1.1 `if` Statements:

Vivid Explanation:

The `if` statement is the most basic conditional statement. It executes a block of code only if a specified condition is true.

Think of it as a gatekeeper: if the condition passes, the code proceeds; otherwise, it's skipped.

Code Examples:

Swift

```
let temperature = 25

if temperature > 20 {
    print("It's a warm day!")
}

let isRaining = false

if !isRaining {
    print("Let's go for a walk.")
}
```

* **Explanation of the Code:**
   * The first `if` statement checks if the `temperature` is greater than 20. If it is, the message "It's a warm day!" is printed.
   * The second if statement checks if isRaining is false. The ! operator reverses the boolean value.

3.1.2 `else` Statements:
Vivid Explanation:

The `else` statement provides an alternative block of code to execute when the `if` statement's condition is false.

It's like having a backup plan: if the first condition doesn't hold, the `else` block takes over.

Code Examples:

Swift

```
let temperature = 15

if temperature > 20 {
```

```
    print("It's a warm day!")
} else {
    print("It's a bit chilly.")
}

let userLoggedIn = false;

if userLoggedIn{
    print("Welcome back user.")
} else {
    print("Please log in.")
}
```

Explanation of the Code:

If the `temperature` is not greater than 20, the message "It's a bit chilly." is printed.

If the user is logged in, then the welcome message is printed, else the login message is printed.

3.1.3 else if Statements:
Vivid Explanation:
The else if statement allows you to check multiple conditions in a sequence. If the if condition is false, the else if conditions are checked in order.

Code Examples:

Swift
```
let score = 85

if score >= 90 {
    print("A")
} else if score >= 80 {
```

```
    print("B")
} else if score >= 70 {
    print("C")
} else {
    print("D or F")
}
```

Explanation of the Code:

The code checks the `score` against multiple ranges and prints the corresponding grade.

3.1.4 `switch` Statements:

Vivid Explanation:

The `switch` statement is a powerful alternative to `if-else if` chains, especially when dealing with multiple possible values. It evaluates an expression and matches its value against multiple cases.

Switch statements are very useful for when you have many different potential values for one variable.

Code Examples:

Swift
```
let dayOfWeek = "Wednesday"

switch dayOfWeek {
case "Monday":
    print("It's the start of the week.")
case "Wednesday":
    print("It's hump day!")
case "Friday":
    print("It's almost the weekend!")
```

```
default:
    print("It's another day.")
}

let number = 3;

switch number {
case 1...3:
    print("Low number")
case 4...6:
    print("Medium number")
default:
    print("High number")
}
```

Explanation of the Code:

The first `switch` statement checks the `dayOfWeek` and prints a message based on the day.

The second switch statement uses a range to determine if the number is low, medium or high.

The `default` case is required to handle any values that don't match the other case

3.1.5 Best Practices:
Vivid Explanation:

Use `if` statements for simple conditions.

Use `else` to provide alternative actions.

Use `else if` for multiple conditions.

Use `switch` for multiple possible values of a single expression.

Ensure that your conditions are clear and concise.

When using switch statements, ensure that all potential values are handled, either by a case, or by the default case.

By covering these aspects, you'll provide your readers with a comprehensive understanding of how to use conditional statements in Swift

3.2 Looping Constructs: For, While, and Repeat-While

Introduction:

Vivid Explanation:

Loops are essential programming constructs that allow you to execute a block of code repeatedly. Swift provides three primary looping constructs: `for`, `while`, and `repeat-while`. Each loop type serves different purposes and offers flexibility in controlling the flow of your program. Understanding these loops is crucial for automating repetitive tasks and processing collections of data.

section will explain how to use these loops effectively to create efficient and concise Swift code.

3.2.1 `for` Loops:

Vivid Explanation

`for` loops are used to iterate over a sequence, such as a range of numbers, an array, or a dictionary. They are ideal for performing a specific task a known number of times

Swift has a few different types of for loops, the most common being the for-in loop.

Code Examples:

Swift
```swift
// Iterating over a range of numbers
for i in 1...5 {
    print("Iteration \(i)")
}

// Iterating over an array
let fruits = ["apple", "banana", "orange"]
for fruit in fruits {
    print("I like \(fruit)")
}

//Iterating over a dictionary
let ages = ["Alice": 30, "Bob": 25, "Charlie": 35]
for (name, age) in ages {
    print("\(name) is \(age) years old")
}
```

* **Explanation of the Code:**
    * The first `for` loop iterates over the range from 1 to 5, printing the iteration number.
    * The second `for` loop iterates over the `fruits` array, printing each fruit.
    * The third `for` loop iterates over the `ages` dictionary, printing each name and age.

3.2.2 while Loops:
Vivid Explanation:

while loops execute a block of code repeatedly as long as a specified condition is true. They are useful when you don't know in advance how many times the loop needs to execute.

Think of a `while` loop as a gate that stays open as long as the condition is met.

Code Examples:
Swift

```
var counter = 0

while counter < 5 {
    print("Counter: \(counter)")
    counter += 1
}

var randomNumber = Int.random(in: 1...10)
var guesses = 0;

while randomNumber != 5 {
    randomNumber = Int.random(in: 1...10);
    guesses += 1;
}

print("It took \(guesses) guesses to get 5.")
```

Explanation of the Code:

The first `while` loop prints the counter value as long as it's less than 5.

The second while loop will guess random numbers until it guesses the number 5.

3.2.3 `repeat-while` Loops:

Vivid Explanation:

`repeat-while` loops are similar to `while` loops, but they guarantee that the loop body is executed at least once. The condition is checked after the loop body is executed.

This is great for when you need to run the code inside the loop at least one time.

Code Examples:
Swift

```swift
var counter = 0

repeat {
    print("Counter: \(counter)")
    counter += 1
} while counter < 5

var diceRoll: Int

repeat {
    diceRoll = Int.random(in: 1...6)
    print("You rolled a \(diceRoll)")
} while diceRoll != 6
```

Explanation of the Code:

The first `repeat-while` loop prints the counter value and increments it until it reaches 5.

The second `repeat-while` loop rolls a dice until it rolls a 6.

3.2.4 Loop Control Statements:

Vivid Explanation:

Swift provides control statements that allow you to modify the behavior of loops. These include break and continue.

break immediately terminates the loop.

continue skips the current iteration and proceeds to the next one.

Code Examples:
Swift
```swift
for i in 1...10 {
    if i == 5 {
        break // Terminate the loop when i is 5
    }
    print(i)
}

for i in 1...10 {
    if i % 2 == 0 {
        continue // Skip even numbers
    }
    print(i)
}
```

Explanation of the Code:

The first `for` loop terminates when `i` reaches 5.

The second `for` loop skips even numbers and prints only odd numbers.

3.2.5 Best Practices:
Vivid Explanation:

Choose the appropriate loop type based on your needs.

Use `for` loops for iterating over sequences.

Use `while` loops for conditions that may change during execution.

Use `repeat-while` loops when you need to execute the loop body at least once.

Use `break` and `continue` to control the flow of your loops.

Avoid infinite loops by ensuring that your loop conditions eventually become false.

3.3 Logical Operators and Decision Making

Introduction:

Vivid Explanation:

Logical operators are the tools that enable your Swift programs to make decisions based on multiple conditions. They allow you to combine and manipulate boolean values, creating complex logical expressions that control the flow of your code. Understanding these operators is crucial for building intelligent and responsive applications.

This section will explain how to use logical operators to create effective decision-making logic in your Swift programs

3.3.1 Logical AND (&&)

Vivid Explanation:

The logical AND operator (&&) returns `true` only if both operands are `true`. If either operand is `false`, the entire expression evaluates to `false`.

Think of it as a strict gatekeeper: both conditions must pass for the gate to open.

Code Examples:
Swift

```swift
let isSunny = true
let isWarm = true

if isSunny && isWarm {
    print("Let's go to the beach!")
}

let age = 25
let hasLicense = true

if age >= 18 && hasLicense {
    print("You are eligible to drive.")
}
```

* **Explanation of the Code:**
    * The first `if` statement checks if both `isSunny` and `isWarm` are `true`.
    * The second `if` statement checks if the `age` is greater than or equal to 18 and `hasLicense` is `true`.

3.3.2 Logical OR (||)

Vivid Explanation:

The logical OR operator (||) returns `true` if at least one operand is `true`. It returns `false` only if both operands are `false`.

Think of it as a lenient gatekeeper: if either condition passes, the gate opens.

Code Examples:
Swift
```
let hasDiscount = true
let isNewCustomer = false

if hasDiscount || isNewCustomer {
    print("You qualify for a special offer!")
}

let isWeekend = true
let hasVacation = false

if isWeekend || hasVacation {
    print("You have free time!")
}
```

* **Explanation of the Code:**
    * The first `if` statement checks if either `hasDiscount` or `isNewCustomer` is `true`.
    * The second `if` statement checks if either `isWeekend` or `hasVacation` is `true`.

3.3.3 Logical NOT (!)

Vivid Explanation:

The logical NOT operator (!) negates a boolean value. If the operand is `true`, it returns `false`, and vice versa.

Think of it as a reverse switch: it flips the state of the condition.

Code Examples:

Swift
```
let isRaining = false

if !isRaining {
    print("It's a clear day.")
}

let isLoggedIn = true

if !isLoggedIn {
    print("Please log in.")
}
```

Explanation of the Code:

The first `if` statement checks if `isRaining` is `false` (i.e., not raining).

The second `if` statement checks if `isLoggedIn` is `false` (i.e., not logged in).

3.3.4 Combining Logical Operators
Vivid Explanation:
You can combine logical operators to create complex logical expressions. Swift evaluates these expressions according to operator precedence, which can be overridden using parentheses.

Parentheses are very useful for clarifying the order of operations.

Code Examples:

Swift
```swift
let temperature = 25
let isSunny = true
let isWeekend = false

if (temperature > 20 && isSunny) || isWeekend {
    print("Let's enjoy the day!")
}

let hasCoupon = true
let isMember = false
let totalSpent = 100

if hasCoupon && (isMember || totalSpent > 50) {
    print("Discount applied!")
}
```

Explanation of the Code:

The first `if` statement checks if it's both warm and sunny, or if it's the weekend.

The second `if` statement checks if the user has a coupon and is either a member or has spent more than $50.

3.3.5 Best Practices:
Vivid Explanation:

Use parentheses to clarify the order of operations in complex expressions.

Keep logical expressions clear and concise.

Avoid overly complex nested conditions.

Use meaningful variable names to improve readability.

Test your logical expressions thoroughly to ensure they behave as expected.

Chapter 4

Functions and Closures

4.1 Defining and Calling Functions

Introduction:

Vivid Explanation:

Functions are fundamental building blocks in Swift that allow you to encapsulate reusable blocks of code. They promote modularity, improve code organization, and reduce redundancy. Defining a function involves specifying its name, parameters, and return type. Calling a function executes the code within its body.

This section will explain how to define and call functions in Swift, covering various aspects such as parameters, return values, and best practices.

4.1.1 Defining Functions:

Vivid Explanation:

In Swift, functions are defined using the `func` keyword, followed by the function name, parameters (if any), and return type (if any). The function body contains the code that will be executed when the function is called.

Think of a function as a mini-program within your program, designed to perform a specific task.

Code Examples:

Swift

```swift
// Function with no parameters and no return value
func greet() {
    print("Hello, world!")
}

// Function with parameters and a return value
func add(a: Int, b: Int) -> Int {
    return a + b
}

//Function with a single parameter and no return.
func printName(name: String){
    print("The name is \(name)")
}
```

Explanation of the Code:

The `greet()` function prints a simple greeting.

The `add(a:b:)` function takes two integer parameters and returns their sum.

The `printName(name:)` function takes a string parameter and prints it

4.1.2 Calling Functions:
Vivid Explanation:
To execute a function, you call it by its name, followed by parentheses. If the function has parameters, you provide the corresponding arguments within the parentheses.

Calling a function is like giving it a command to perform its designated task.

Code Examples:

Swift

```
greet() // Calls the greet() function

    let sum = add(a: 5, b: 3) // Calls the add() function and stores
the result
    print("Sum: \(sum)") // Output: Sum: 8

    printName(name: "John Doe") //Calls the printName function.
```

Explanation of the Code:

The `greet()` function is called without any arguments.

The `add()` function is called with arguments 5 and 3, and the result is stored in the `sum` constant.

The `printName()` function is called with the argument "John Doe".

4.1.3 Function Parameters and Arguments:

Vivid Explanation:

Parameters are the placeholders for values that a function expects to receive. Arguments are the actual values that are passed to the function when it is called.

Parameters are like the input slots of a machine, and arguments are the items that are inserted into those slots.

Code Examples:

Swift

```swift
func multiply(number: Int, by multiplier: Int) -> Int {
    return number * multiplier
}

let result = multiply(number: 10, by: 2)
print("Result: \(result)") // Output: Result: 20
```

Explanation of the Code:

The `multiply()` function has two parameters: `number` and `multiplier`.

The function is called with arguments 10 and 2.

4.1.4 Function Return Values
Vivid Explanation:

Functions can return values to the caller using the `->` syntax, followed by the return type. If a function doesn't return a value, its return type is Void (or omitted).

A function can send back a result, like a machine delivering a finished product.

Code Examples:

Swift

```swift
func isEven(number: Int) -> Bool {
    return number % 2 == 0
}

let numberToCheck = 7
```

```
if isEven(number: numberToCheck) {
    print("\(numberToCheck) is even.")
} else {
    print("\(numberToCheck) is odd.")
}
```

Explanation of the Code:

The `isEven()` function returns a boolean value indicating whether the input number is even.

The `if` statement uses the return value to determine the output

4.1.5 Best Practices
Vivid Explanation:
Use descriptive function names.

Keep functions focused on a single task.

Use parameters to make functions flexible.

Return values to provide results to the caller.

Use comments to document function purpose and usage.

4.2 Understanding Function Parameters and Return Values

Introduction:

Vivid Explanation:

Function parameters and return values are the communication channels between a function and the rest of your code. Parameters are the inputs a function receives, and return values are the outputs it produces. Mastering these concepts is essential for creating versatile and reusable functions.

This section will explore the different types of parameters, how to define them, and how to work with return values effectively.

4.2.1 Function Parameters:

Vivid Explanation:

Function parameters are the variables declared within the function's parentheses, acting as placeholders for the values that will be passed into the function when it's called. They allow functions to operate on different data without needing to be rewritten.

Think of parameters as the ingredients a chef requests to cook a specific dish.

Code Examples:

Swift
```
func calculateArea(width: Double, height: Double) -> Double {
    return width * height
```

```
}

let roomArea = calculateArea(width: 10.0, height: 5.0)
print("Room area: \(roomArea)") // Output: Room area: 50.0

func greet(person: String, withGreeting: String = "Hello") {
    print("\(withGreeting), \(person)!")
}

greet(person: "Alice") //Uses default parameter.
    greet(person: "Bob", withGreeting: "Hi") //Overrides default
parameter.
```

Explanation of the Code:

The `calculateArea()` function takes two `Double` parameters, `width` and `height`, and returns their product.

The `greet()` function takes a `person` string parameter and a `withGreeting` string parameter with a default value of "Hello".

4.2.2 Argument Labels and Parameter Names:

Vivid Explanation:

Swift distinguishes between argument labels and parameter names. Argument labels are used when calling the function, while parameter names are used within the function's body. This allows for more readable function calls.

Argument labels are like the instructions on a form, and parameter names are the internal variables used to process the information.

Code Examples:

Swift

```swift
func power(base: Int, toThe exponent: Int) -> Int {
    var result = 1
    for _ in 0..<exponent {
        result *= base
    }
    return result
}

let result = power(base: 2, toThe: 3)
print("2 to the power of 3 is: \(result)") // Output: 2 to the power
```
of 3 is: 8

Explanation of the Code:

The `power()` function uses `toThe` as an argument label, making the function call more readable

4.2.3 Variadic Parameters

Vivid Explanation:

Variadic parameters allow a function to accept a variable number of arguments of the same type. They are denoted by three dots (. . .) after the parameter type

Think of variadic parameters as a flexible container that can hold any number of items

Code Examples:

Swift

```swift
func calculateSum(numbers: Int...) -> Int {
    var total = 0
```

```swift
    for number in numbers {
        total += number
    }
    return total
}

let sum = calculateSum(numbers: 1, 2, 3, 4, 5)
print("Sum: \(sum)") // Output: Sum: 15
```

Explanation of the Code:

The `calculateSum()` function accepts any number of `Int` arguments and returns their sum.

4.2.4 Function Return Values:
Vivid Explanation:

Function return values are the results that a function sends back to the caller. They allow functions to produce outputs that can be used in other parts of your code.

Return values are like the finished product a machine delivers after processing the inputs.

Code Examples:

Swift
```swift
func getFullName(firstName: String, lastName: String) -> String {
    return "\(firstName) \(lastName)"
}

let fullName = getFullName(firstName: "John", lastName: "Doe")
print("Full name: \(fullName)") // Output: Full name: John Doe

func divide(a: Double, b: Double) -> Double? {
```

```
    if b == 0 {
        return nil
    }
    return a / b
}

if let result = divide(a: 10.0, b: 2.0) {
    print("Division result: \(result)") //Output: Division result: 5.0
} else {
    print("Cannot divide by zero.")
}
```

Explanation of the Code:

The `getFullName()` function returns a `String` representing the full name.

The `divide()` function returns an optional `Double` to handle division by zero

4.2.5 Best Practices:
Vivid Explanation:

Use clear and descriptive parameter names and argument labels.

Use default parameters to provide flexibility.

Use variadic parameters when you need to accept a variable number of arguments.

Return appropriate values to provide meaningful results.

Use optionals to handle cases where a function may not be able to return a value.

By covering these aspects, you'll provide your readers with a comprehensive understanding of function parameters and return values in Swift.

4.3 Working with Closures: Anonymous Functions

Introduction:

Vivid Explanation:

Closures are self-contained blocks of functionality that can be passed around and used in your code. They are similar to[1] anonymous functions in other languages, allowing you to create inline blocks of code without explicitly defining a named function. Closures are powerful tools for writing concise and flexible Swift code.

This section will explain how to define and use closures, covering various aspects such as closure syntax, capturing values, and trailing closures

4.3.1 Closure Syntax:

Vivid Explanation:

Closures in Swift have a concise syntax that allows you to define them inline. The general syntax is: `{ (parameters) -> return type in statements }`. Think of closures as mini, portable functions that you can create and use on the fly.

Code Examples:

Swift

```swift
// A simple closure that adds two numbers
let add: (Int, Int) -> Int = { (a, b) in
    return a + b
}

let sum = add(10, 5)
print("Sum: \(sum)") // Output: Sum: 15

// A closure that prints a message
let printMessage: () -> Void = {
    print("This is a closure message.")
}

printMessage() // Output: This is a closure message.
```

Explanation of the Code:

The `add` closure takes two `Int` parameters and returns their sum.

The `printMessage` closure takes no parameters and returns `Void`, printing a message.

4.3.2 Shorthand Argument Names
Vivid Explanation:

Swift provides shorthand argument names for inline closures, allowing you to refer to the parameters by their position ($0, $1, $2, etc.). This can make closures even more concise.

Shorthand argument names are like quick references to the inputs of your mini-functions.

Code Examples:

Swift

```
let multiply: (Int, Int) -> Int = {
    return $0 * $1
}

let product = multiply(3, 4)
print("Product: \(product)") // Output: Product: 12

let sortArray: ([Int]) -> [Int] = {
    return $0.sorted()
}

let sortedNumbers = sortArray([5, 2, 8, 1])
print("Sorted Numbers: \(sortedNumbers)") //Output: [1, 2, 5, 8]
```

Explanation of the Code:

The `multiply` closure uses `$0` and `$1` to refer to the first and second parameters.

The `sortArray` closure uses `$0` to refer to the input array.

4.3.3 Implicit Returns from Single-Expression Closures:

Vivid Explanation:

If a closure contains a single expression, you can omit the `return` keyword, and Swift will implicitly return the result of the expression.

Implicit returns are like automatic deliveries of the result from your mini-functions.

Code Examples:

Swift

```
let square: (Int) -> Int = { $0 * $0 }

let squaredValue = square(5)
    print("Squared Value: \(squaredValue)") // Output: Squared
Value: 25
```

Explanation of the Code:

The `square` closure implicitly returns the square of the input parameter.

4.3.4 Trailing Closures:

Vivid Explanation:

If a closure is the last argument of a function, you can write it outside the function's parentheses as a trailing closure. This makes the code more readable, especially for longer closures.

Trailing closures are like attaching a separate instruction sheet to a function call.

Code Examples:

Swift

```
func performOperation(a: Int, b: Int, operation: (Int, Int) -> Int) ->
Int {
    return operation(a, b)
}

let result = performOperation(a: 10, b: 5) { $0 - $1 }
print("Result: \(result)") // Output: Result: 5

let numbers = [1,2,3,4,5]
```

```
let evenNumbers = numbers.filter { $0 % 2 == 0}
print("Even numbers: \(evenNumbers)") //Output: [2,4]
```

Explanation of the Code:

The `performOperation` function takes a closure as its last argument, which is provided as a trailing closure.

The filter function uses a trailing closure to determine if a number is even.

4.3.5 Capturing Values:
Vivid Explanation:

Closures can capture values from their surrounding context, even if the context goes out of scope. This allows closures to retain and use variables from their enclosing functions.

Capturing values is like a closure taking snapshots of its environment

Code Examples:

Swift
```
func makeIncrementer(incrementAmount: Int) -> () -> Int {
    var runningTotal = 0
    return {
        runningTotal += incrementAmount
        return runningTotal
    }
}

let incrementByTen = makeIncrementer(incrementAmount: 10)
print(incrementByTen()) // Output: 10
print(incrementByTen()) // Output: 20
```

Explanation of the Code:

The `makeIncrementer` function returns a closure that captures the `runningTotal` and `incrementAmount` variables

4.3.6 Best Practices:
Vivid Explanation:

Use closures to create concise and reusable code blocks.

Use shorthand argument names and implicit returns to make closures more compact.

Use trailing closures to improve readability.

Be mindful of capturing values to avoid unintended side effects.

By covering these aspects, you'll provide your readers with a comprehensive understanding of how to work with closures in Swift.

Chapter 5

Structures and Classes

5.1 Defining Structures and Classes

Introduction:

Vivid Explanation:

Structures and classes are fundamental building blocks in Swift that allow you to define custom data types. They encapsulate properties (data) and methods (functions) into a single unit, enabling you to create complex and organized data models. Understanding the differences and similarities between structures and classes is crucial for effective Swift development.

This section will explain how to define structures and classes, covering various aspects such as properties, methods, and their key differences.

5.1.1 Defining Structures:

Vivid Explanation:

Structures are value types in Swift, meaning that when a structure instance is assigned to a variable or constant, or when it's passed to a function, a copy of that instance is created.[1] Structures are ideal for representing simple data values.

Think of structures as blueprints for creating lightweight, value-based objects.

Code Examples:

Swift

```swift
struct Point {
    var x: Int
    var y: Int

    func describe() -> String {
        return "Point(x: \(x), y: \(y))"
    }
}


let myPoint = Point(x: 10, y: 20)
print(myPoint.describe()) // Output: Point(x: 10, y: 20)

var anotherPoint = myPoint;
anotherPoint.x = 30;
print(myPoint.x) //Output: 10
print(anotherPoint.x) //Output: 30
```

Explanation of the Code:

The `Point` structure defines two integer properties, `x` and `y`, and a method `describe()` that returns a string description of the point.

When anotherPoint is created, it is a copy of myPoint. Therefore, changing anotherPoint does not change myPoint.

5.1.2 Defining Classes:

Vivid Explanation:
Classes are reference types in Swift, meaning that when a class instance is assigned to a variable or constant, or when it's passed to a function, a reference to that instance is created.[2] Classes are

ideal for representing complex data models and objects with identity.

Think of classes as blueprints for creating more complex, reference-based objects.

Code Examples:

Swift
```
class Person {
    var name: String
    var age: Int

    init(name: String, age: Int) {
        self.name = name
        self.age = age
    }

    func introduce() {
        print("My name is \(name) and I am \(age) years old.")
    }
}

let john = Person(name: "John", age: 30)
john.introduce() // Output: My name is John and I am 30 years old.

let anotherPerson = john;
anotherPerson.name = "Jane";
john.introduce() //Output: My name is Jane and I am 30 years old.
```

Explanation of the Code:

The `Person` class defines two properties, `name` and `age`, an initializer `init()`, and a method `introduce()`.

Because classes are reference types, anotherPerson points to the same object as john. Therefore, changing anotherPerson changes john.

5.1.3 Properties:
Vivid Explanation:

Properties are variables and constants that are stored as part of a structure or class.[3] They represent the data associated with an instance of the type.

Properties are like the attributes or characteristics of an object.

Code Examples:

Swift
```
struct Rectangle {
    var width: Double
    var height: Double

    var area: Double {
        return width * height
    }
}

let myRectangle = Rectangle(width: 5.0, height: 10.0)
print("Area: \(myRectangle.area)") // Output: Area: 50.0
```

Explanation of the Code:

The `Rectangle` structure has stored properties `width` and `height`, and a computed property `area`.

5.1.4 Methods:

Vivid Explanation:

Methods are functions that are associated with a structure or class.[4] They define the behavior of an instance of the type.

Methods are like the actions or operations that an object can perform.

Code Examples:

Swift
```swift
class Counter {
    var count = 0

    func increment() {
        count += 1
    }
}

let myCounter = Counter()
myCounter.increment()
print("Count: \(myCounter.count)") // Output: Count: 1
```

Explanation of the Code:

The `Counter` class has a method `increment()` that increments the `count` property.

5.1.5 Key Differences:
Vivid Explanation:

Structures are value types, and classes are reference types.[5]

Classes support inheritance, structures do not.

Classes have deinitializers, structures do not.[6]

Classes do not have an automatically generated memberwise initializer, Structures do.

Best Practices:
Use structures for simple data values.

Use classes for complex data models and objects with identity.

Choose appropriate property and method names.

Use initializers to set up instances of structures and classes.

By covering these aspects, you'll provide your readers with a comprehensive understanding of how to define structures and classes in Swift.

5.2 Properties and Methods: Building Objects

Introduction:

Vivid Explanation:

Properties and methods are the core components of structures and classes, enabling you to build complex and interactive objects. Properties store data, while methods define behavior. Together, they allow you to create objects that model real-world entities and perform specific tasks.

This section will explain how to define and use properties and methods, covering various aspects such as stored properties, computed properties, instance methods, and type methods.

5.2.1 Stored Properties:

Vivid Explanation:

Stored properties are variables or constants that are stored as part of an instance of a structure or class. They hold the data associated with the instance.

Think of stored properties as the attributes or characteristics that an object possesses.

Code Examples:

Swift
```
struct Book {
    var title: String
    var author: String
    let publicationYear: Int // Constant stored property
}

let myBook = Book(title: "The Swift Handbook", author: "John Smith", publicationYear: 2023)
    print("Title: \(myBook.title), Author: \(myBook.author), Year: \(myBook.publicationYear)")
```

Explanation of the Code:

The `Book` structure has three stored properties: `title`, `author`, and `publicationYear`.

`publicationYear` is a constant property, so its value cannot be changed after initialization.

5.2.2 Computed Properties:
Vivid Explanation:

Computed properties do not store values directly. Instead, they provide a getter and an optional setter to retrieve and set other properties and values indirectly.

Think of computed properties as dynamic values that are calculated on demand

Code Examples:

```swift
Swift
  struct Circle {
    var radius: Double
    var diameter: Double {
      get {
        return radius * 2
      }
      set {
        radius = newValue / 2
      }
    }
    var area: Double {
      return Double.pi * radius * radius
    }
  }

  var myCircle = Circle(radius: 5.0)
  print("Diameter: \(myCircle.diameter), Area: \(myCircle.area)") //
Output: Diameter: 10.0, Area: 78.53981633974483
  myCircle.diameter = 20.0;
```

print("Radius: \(myCircle.radius)") //Output: 10.0

Explanation of the Code:

The `Circle` structure has a stored property `radius` and computed properties `diameter` and `area`.

The `diameter` computed property has a getter and a setter, while `area` has only a getter.

5.2.3 Instance Methods:

Vivid Explanation:

Instance methods are functions that are associated with an instance of a structure or class. They can access and modify the instance's properties.

Think of instance methods as the actions that an individual object can perform.

Code Examples:

Swift
```
class Counter {
    var count = 0

    func increment() {
        count += 1
    }

    func increment(by amount: Int) {
        count += amount
    }
```

```swift
    func reset() {
        count = 0
    }
}
```

```swift
let myCounter = Counter()
myCounter.increment()
myCounter.increment(by: 3)
print("Count: \(myCounter.count)") // Output: Count: 4
myCounter.reset()
print("Count: \(myCounter.count)") //Output: Count: 0
```

Explanation of the Code:

The `Counter` class has instance methods `increment()`, `increment(by:)`, and `reset()`.

5.2.4 Type Methods:
Vivid Explanation:

Type methods are functions that are associated with the type itself, rather than an instance of the type. They are called on the type using the static or class keyword.

Think of type methods as actions that the type itself can perform, rather than individual objects.

Code Examples:

Swift
```swift
struct Math {
    static func square(number: Int) -> Int {
        return number * number
    }
}
```

```
let squaredValue = Math.square(number: 7)
    print("Squared Value: \(squaredValue)") // Output: Squared
Value: 49

class Logger{
    static func logMessage(message: String){
       print("Log: \(message)")
    }
}

Logger.logMessage(message: "App started")
```

Explanation of the Code:

The `Math` structure has a type method `square(number:)`.

The `Logger` class has a type method `logMessage(message:)`.

5.2.5 Mutating Methods:

Vivid Explanation:

Structures are value types, so their properties cannot be modified within instance methods by default. To modify a structure's properties, you need to declare the method as mutating.

Mutating methods allow structures to change their internal state.

Code Examples:

Swift
```
struct Point {
    var x: Int
    var y: Int
```

```swift
    mutating func move(x: Int, y: Int) {
        self.x += x
        self.y += y
    }
}

var myPoint = Point(x: 10, y: 20)
myPoint.move(x: 5, y: 10)
    print("Point: (\(myPoint.x), \(myPoint.y))") // Output: Point: (15,
30)
```

Explanation of the Code:

The `Point` structure has a mutating method `move(x:y:)` that modifies the `x` and `y` properties.

5.2.6 Best Practices:
Vivid Explanation:

Use stored properties to hold data.

Use computed properties to calculate values on demand.

Use instance methods to define object behavior.

Use type methods to define type-level behavior.

Use mutating methods to modify structure properties.

Choose appropriate property and method names.

By covering these aspects, you'll provide your readers with a comprehensive understanding of how to use properties and methods to build objects in Swift.

5.3   Inheritance   and   Polymorphism: Object-Oriented Principles

Introduction:

Vivid Explanation:

Inheritance and polymorphism are two fundamental pillars of object-oriented programming (OOP) that promote code reuse and flexibility. Inheritance allows you to create new classes based on existing ones, inheriting their properties and methods. Polymorphism allows objects of different classes to be treated as objects of a common superclass. Together, they enable you to build robust and maintainable applications.

This section will explain how to use inheritance and polymorphism in Swift, covering various aspects such as subclassing, overriding, and type casting.

5.3.1 Inheritance:

Vivid Explanation:

Inheritance allows you to create a new class (subclass or derived class) based on an existing class (superclass or base class). The subclass inherits the[1] properties and methods of the superclass, and you can add new properties and methods or override existing ones.

Think of inheritance as creating a specialized version of an existing object, inheriting its core characteristics.

Code Examples:

Swift

```swift
class Vehicle {
    var currentSpeed = 0.0
    var description: String {
        return "Traveling at \(currentSpeed) miles per hour"
    }
    func makeNoise() {
        print("Vroom!")
    }
}

class Car: Vehicle {
    var gear = 1
    override var description: String {
        return super.description + " in gear \(gear)"
    }
    override func makeNoise() {
        print("Honk Honk!")
    }
}

let myCar = Car()
myCar.currentSpeed = 25.0
myCar.gear = 2
print(myCar.description) // Output: Traveling at 25.0 miles per hour in gear 2
myCar.makeNoise() // Output: Honk Honk!
```

Explanation of the Code:

The `Car` class inherits from the `Vehicle` class.

The `Car` class overrides the `description` property and the `makeNoise()` method.

The `super` keyword is used to access the superclass's implementation

5.3.2 Subclassing and Overriding:

Vivid Explanation:

Subclassing is the process of creating a new class based on an existing class. Overriding is the process of providing a new implementation for a property or method in a subclass

Subclassing extends the functionality of a superclass, while overriding modifies its behavior

Code Examples:

Swift
```
class Bicycle: Vehicle {
    override func makeNoise() {
        print("Ring Ring!")
    }
}

let myBicycle = Bicycle()
myBicycle.makeNoise() // Output: Ring Ring!
```

Explanation of the Code:

The `Bicycle` class inherits from the `Vehicle` class and overrides the `makeNoise()` method.

5.3.3 Polymorphism:

Vivid Explanation:

Polymorphism allows objects of different classes to be treated as objects of a common superclass. This enables you to write code that can work[2] with objects of various types in a uniform manner.

Think of polymorphism as the ability of objects to take on multiple forms.

Code Examples:
Swift

```
let vehicles: [Vehicle] = [Car(), Bicycle(), Vehicle()]

for vehicle in vehicles {
    vehicle.makeNoise()
}
//Output: Honk Honk!
//Output: Ring Ring!
//Output: Vroom!
```

Explanation of the Code:

The `vehicles` array contains objects of different subclasses of `Vehicle`.

The `makeNoise()` method is called on each object, and the appropriate implementation is executed based on the object's type.

5.3.4 Type Casting
Vivid Explanation:

Type casting allows you to check and convert the type of an object at runtime. Swift provides two type casting operators: as? (conditional type cast) and as! (forced type cast).

Type casting is like checking the label on a box and then transforming its contents.

Code Examples:
Swift
```
  if let car = vehicles[0] as? Car {
     print("This vehicle is a car, gear: \(car.gear)")
  }

  if vehicles[1] is Bicycle {
     print("This vehicle is a bicycle")
  }
```

Explanation of the Code:

The `as?` operator attempts to cast `vehicles[0]` to a `Car` object.

The `is` operator checks if `vehicles[1]` is a `Bicycle` object.

5.3.5 Best Practices:
Vivid Explanation:

Use inheritance to create specialized versions of existing classes.

Use overriding to modify the behavior of superclass properties and methods

Use polymorphism to write code that can work with objects of various types.

Use type casting to check and convert the type of an object at runtime.

Design your class hierarchies carefully to promote code reuse and maintainability.

Chapter 6

Optionals and Error Handling

6.1 Understanding Optionals: Handling Null Values

Introduction:

Vivid Explanation:

In Swift, optionals are a powerful feature that allows you to handle the absence of a value. They are essential for dealing with situations where a variable or constant might not have a value, preventing runtime errors and making your code more robust. Understanding optionals is crucial for writing safe and reliable Swift code.

This section will explain what optionals are, how to declare and use them, and the various techniques for unwrapping optional values.

6.1.1 What Are Optionals?

Vivid Explanation:

An optional is a type that can hold either a value or `nil`, which represents the absence of a value. It's like a box that may or may not contain something. Optionals are denoted by adding a question mark (`?`) after the type.

Think of optionals as a way to handle uncertainty in your code, acknowledging that a value might not always be present.

Code Examples:

Swift
```
var optionalString: String? // Declares an optional String
optionalString = "Hello, Swift!"
optionalString = nil // Assigns nil to the optional
```

Explanation of the Code:

`optionalString` is declared as an optional `String`, which can hold either a string value or `nil`.

We assign a string value to `optionalString` and then assign `nil` to it

6.1.2 Optional Binding
Vivid Explanation:

Optional binding is a technique for checking if an optional contains a value and, if it does, extracting that value into a constant or variable. It uses the `if let` or `if var` syntax.

Optional binding is like safely opening the optional box and checking if it contains something

Code Examples:

Swift
```
var optionalNumber: Int? = 42

if let number = optionalNumber {
    print("Optional number has a value: \(number)")
} else {
```

```
    print("Optional number is nil.")
  }
```

Explanation of the Code:

The `if let` statement checks if `optionalNumber` has a value.

If it does, the value is extracted into the `number` constant, and the `if` block is executed.

If it is nil, the else block is executed.

6.1.3 Forced Unwrapping:
Vivid Explanation:

Forced unwrapping is a technique for extracting the value from an optional using the force unwrap operator (`!`). However, if the optional is `nil`, forced unwrapping will cause a runtime error.

Forced unwrapping is like forcefully opening the optional box, assuming it contains something, which can be risky.

Code Examples:

Swift
```
  var optionalValue: String? = "Swift"

  if optionalValue != nil {
    let unwrappedValue = optionalValue!
    print("Unwrapped value: \(unwrappedValue)")
  }
```

Explanation of the Code

The `if` statement checks if `optionalValue` is not `nil`.

If it's not `nil`, the force unwrap operator (`!`) is used to extract the value.

Warning. Never force unwrap an optional if you are not 100% sure that it contains a value.

6.1.4 Nil-Coalescing Operator:

Vivid Explanation:

The nil-coalescing operator (??) provides a default value for an optional if it's `nil`. It's a concise way to handle optional values with a fallback

The nil-coalescing operator is like having a backup plan in case the optional box is empty.

Code Examples:

Swift
```
var optionalName: String?
let name = optionalName ?? "Guest"
print("Name: \(name)") // Output: Name: Guest

optionalName = "Alice"
let anotherName = optionalName ?? "Guest"
print("Name: \(anotherName)") //Output: Name: Alice
```

Explanation of the Code:

If `optionalName` is `nil`, the nil-coalescing operator returns "Guest".

If `optionalName` has a value, it returns that value.

6.1.5 Optional Chaining:
Vivid Explanation:

Optional chaining is a technique for accessing properties and methods of an optional that might be `nil`. It allows you to safely access nested properties and methods without causing runtime errors.

Optional chaining is like a safe path through a series of optional boxes, stopping if any box is empty.

Code Examples:
Swift
```
  class Person {
      var residence: Residence?
  }

  class Residence {
      var numberOfRooms = 1
  }

  let john = Person()
  let roomCount = john.residence?.numberOfRooms
  print("Room Count: \(roomCount)") // Output: Room Count: nil

  john.residence = Residence()
  let updatedRoomCount = john.residence?.numberOfRooms
      print("Room Count: \(updatedRoomCount)") //Output: Room
Count: Optional(1)
```

Explanation of the Code:

The `john.residence?.numberOfRooms` expression attempts to access the `numberOfRooms` property of `john.residence`.

If `john.residence` is `nil`, the expression returns `nil`.

6.1.6 Best Practices:

Vivid Explanation:
Use optionals to handle the absence of values.

Use optional binding to safely unwrap optionals.

Avoid forced unwrapping unless absolutely necessary.

Use the nil-coalescing operator to provide default values.

Use optional chaining to safely access nested properties and methods.

By covering these aspects, you'll provide your readers with a comprehensive understanding of how to work with optionals in Swift.

6.2 Optional Binding and Forced Unwrapping

Introduction:

Vivid Explanation:

Optionals in Swift are a powerful tool for handling the potential absence of a value.[1] However, extracting the value from an optional requires careful handling. Optional binding and forced unwrapping are two techniques for doing this, but they have significant differences in terms of safety and error handling.

This section will explain how to use optional binding and forced unwrapping, highlighting their differences and best practices.

6.2.1 Optional Binding (if let/if var):

Vivid Explanation:

Optional binding is a safe and preferred way to unwrap optionals.[2] It checks if an optional contains a value and, if it does, extracts that value into a constant or variable within a conditional block.[3]

Think of optional binding as a cautious approach, checking if the optional box contains something before attempting to access it.

Code Examples:

Swift

```
var optionalName: String? = "Alice"

if let name = optionalName {
    print("The name is \(name)") // Executes if optionalName has
a value
} else {
    print("Name is nil") // Executes if optionalName is nil
}

var optionalAge: Int? = 30;

if var age = optionalAge {
    age += 1;
    print("The age is \(age)")
}
```

Explanation of the Code:

The `if let name = optionalName` statement checks if `optionalName` has a value.

If it does, the value is assigned to the constant `name`, and the code within the `if` block is executed.

If a var is used, then the value is able to be modified within the if statement

6.2.2 Forced Unwrapping (!):

Vivid Explanation:
Forced unwrapping uses the force unwrap operator (!) to extract the value from an optional. However, if the optional is nil, forced unwrapping will cause a runtime error, crashing your application.

Forced unwrapping is like a risky gamble, assuming the optional box always contains something, which can lead to crashes.

Code Examples:
Swift

```
var optionalNumber: Int? = 10

    // Only use forced unwrapping if you're absolutely sure the optional has a value!
    if optionalNumber != nil {
        let number = optionalNumber!
        print("The number is \(number)")
    }

    var dangerousOptional: String?
```

```
//let dangerousString = dangerousOptional! //This will cause a
crash.
```

Explanation of the Code:

The `optionalNumber!` expression forcefully extracts the value
from `optionalNumber`.

The commented out code will cause a crash, because
dangerousOptional is nil.

Warning: Avoid forced unwrapping whenever possible. Use it only
when you are absolutely certain that the optional has a value

6.2.3 Differences and Best Practices:
Vivid Explanation:

Optional binding is safe and prevents runtime errors, while forced
unwrapping is risky and can cause crashes.[4]

Always prefer optional binding over forced unwrapping.

Use forced unwrapping only in situations where you are absolutely
certain that the optional has a value, such as when you initialize a
variable with a value that will always be present

If you're unsure whether an optional has a value, use optional
binding or the nil-coalescing operator (??) to provide a default
value.

Key Differences:
Safety: Optional binding is safe, forced unwrapping is unsafe

Error Handling: Optional binding handles nil gracefully, forced
unwrapping crashes on nil.

Readability: Optional binding is more readable and conveys intent clearly.[6]

By emphasizing the importance of safe optional handling, you'll equip your readers with the knowledge to write robust and error-free Swift code.

6.3 Error Handling with Try, Catch, and Throw

Introduction:

Vivid Explanation:

Error handling is a crucial aspect of writing robust and reliable Swift code. It allows you to gracefully manage unexpected situations and prevent your application from crashing. Swift provides a powerful error handling mechanism using the `try`, `catch`, and `throw` keywords.

This section will explain how to define and throw errors, how to handle errors using `try` and `catch`, and best practices for error handling in Swift.

6.3.1 Defining Errors:

Vivid Explanation:

In Swift, errors are represented by types that conform to the `Error` protocol. You can define custom error types using enums, which are particularly well-suited for representing a set of related errors.

Think of error types as labels for different kinds of problems that can occur.

   ○ **Code Examples:**

Swift

```swift
enum DataError: Error {
    case fileNotFound
    case invalidData
    case networkError
}
```

* **Explanation of the Code:**
    * The `DataError` enum defines three possible error cases: `fileNotFound`, `invalidData`, and `networkError`.

6.3.2 Throwing Errors:

Vivid Explanation:
Functions or methods that can throw errors are marked with the `throws` keyword. When an error occurs, you can use the `throw` keyword to propagate the error.

Throwing an error is like signaling that something went wrong and passing the problem to the caller.

Code Examples:
Swift

```swift
func fetchData(from file: String) throws -> String {
    guard file == "data.txt" else {
        throw DataError.fileNotFound
    }

    // Simulate reading data
    let data = "Some valid data"
    return data
}
```

Explanation of the Code:

The `fetchData(from:)` function is marked with `throws`, indicating that it can throw an error.

The `guard` statement checks if the file name is "data.txt". If not, it throws a `DataError.fileNotFound` error.

6.3.3 Handling Errors with `try` and `catch`:
Vivid Explanation:

To handle errors, you use the `try` keyword to call a throwing function or method. The `try` keyword can be used in three ways: `try`, `try?`, and `try!`.

`try`: Executes the throwing function and propagates the error if it occurs.

`try?`: Executes the throwing function and returns an optional value. If an error occurs, it returns `nil`.

`try!`: Executes the throwing function and forcefully unwraps the result. If an error occurs, it crashes the application.

Code Examples:

Swift
```
do {
    let data = try fetchData(from: "data.txt")
    print("Data: \(data)")
} catch DataError.fileNotFound {
    print("Error: File not found.")
} catch DataError.invalidData {
    print("Error: Invalid data.")
```

```
} catch {
    print("An unknown error occurred.")
}

if let data = try? fetchData(from: "data.txt") {
    print("Data: \(data)")
} else {
    print("Error occurred while fetching data.")
}

// try! fetchData(from: "data.txt") // Use with caution!
```

Explanation of the Code:

The `do-catch` block attempts to execute `fetchData(from:)`. If an error occurs, the corresponding `catch` block is executed.

The `try?` expression attempts to execute `fetchData(from:)`. If an error occurs, it returns `nil`.

The commented out `try!` will crash the application if an error is thrown.

6.3.4 Error Propagation:
Vivid Explanation:

Errors can be propagated up the call stack until they are handled. This allows you to handle errors at the appropriate level of abstraction.

Error propagation is like passing a problem up the chain of command until someone can solve it.

Code Examples:

Swift

```swift
func processData(file: String) throws {
    let data = try fetchData(from: file)
    // Process data
    print("Data processed: \(data)")
}

do {
    try processData(file: "data.txt")
} catch {
    print("Error processing data: \(error)")
}
```

Explanation of the Code:

The `processData(file:)` function throws any errors that occur during the `fetchData(from:)` call

6.3.5 Best Practice

Vivid Explanation:
Define custom error types using enums to represent specific error conditions.

Use `throws` to mark functions and methods that can throw errors.

Use `try` and `catch` to handle errors gracefully.

Use `try?` to handle errors when you're not interested in the specific error details.

Avoid `try!` unless you are absolutely certain that an error will not occur.

Propagate errors up the call stack to handle them at the appropriate level.

Provide informative error messages to help with debugging.

By covering these aspects, you'll provide your readers with a comprehensive understanding of how to use error handling in Swift.

Chapter 7

Collections: Arrays, Dictionaries, and Sets

7.1 Working with Arrays: Ordered Collections

Introduction:

Vivid Explanation:

Arrays are ordered collections of values of the same type. They are fundamental data structures in Swift, allowing you to store and manage lists of items. Arrays are versatile and widely used in various programming tasks, from storing lists of names to managing complex data sets.

This section will explain how to create, access, modify, and iterate over arrays in Swift, covering various aspects such as array initialization, adding and removing elements, and array operations.

7.1.1 Creating Arrays:

Vivid Explanation:

You can create arrays in Swift using various methods, including array literals, initializers, and type annotations.

Think of arrays as ordered lists, where each item has a specific position or index.

Code Examples:

Swift
```
  // Array literal
  let numbers = [1, 2, 3, 4, 5]

  // Empty array with type annotation
  var names: [String] = []

  // Array initializer
  let zeros = Array(repeating: 0, count: 10)
```

Explanation of the Code:

The `numbers` array is created using an array literal.

The `names` array is created as an empty array of strings.

The `zeros` array is created using the `Array(repeating:count:)` initializer.

7.1.2 Accessing Array Elements:
Vivid Explanation:

You can access array elements using their index, which starts at 0 for the first element.

Think of indices as the addresses of items in the array, allowing you to retrieve specific items.

Code Examples:

Swift
```
  let fruits = ["apple", "banana", "orange"]

  let firstFruit = fruits[0] // Accesses the first element
  let secondFruit = fruits[1] // Accesses the second element
```

```swift
print("First fruit: \(firstFruit)")
print("Second fruit: \(secondFruit)")
```

Explanation of the Code:

fruits[0]` accesses the first element ("apple").

fruits[1]` accesses the second element ("banana").

7.1.3 Modifying Arrays:

Vivid Explanation:
You can modify arrays by adding, removing, or changing elements.
Swift provides various methods for these operations.

Modifying arrays is like updating the contents of a list, adding,
removing, or changing items as needed.

Code Examples:
Swift
```swift
  var colors = ["red", "green", "blue"]

  // Adding elements
  colors.append("yellow")
  colors += ["purple", "white"]

  // Inserting elements
  colors.insert("cyan", at: 2)

  // Removing elements
  colors.remove(at: 1)
  colors.removeLast()

  // Changing elements
```

```swift
colors[0] = "magenta"

print("Colors: \(colors)")
```

Explanation of the Code:

append()` adds an element to the end of the array.

insert(at:)` inserts an element at a specific index.

remove(at:)` removes an element at a specific index.

removeLast()` removes the last element.

colors[0] = "magenta"` changes the first element.

7.1.4 Iterating Over Arrays:
Vivid Explanation:
You can iterate over arrays using `for-in` loops, allowing you to process each element in the array.

Iterating over arrays is like going through each item in a list, one by one, and performing an action.

Code Examples:

Swift
```swift
let numbers = [10, 20, 30, 40, 50]

for number in numbers {
    print("Number: \(number)")
}

for (index, number) in numbers.enumerated() {
    print("Index: \(index), Number: \(number)")
```

```
    }
```

Explanation of the Code:

The first `for-in` loop iterates over each element in the `numbers` array.

The second `for-in` loop uses `enumerated()` to get both the index and the element.

7.1.5 Array Operations:
Vivid Explanation:
Swift provides various array operations, such as filtering, mapping, and sorting, which allow you to manipulate arrays efficiently.

Array operations are like tools for transforming and manipulating lists, allowing you to perform complex tasks with ease.

Code Examples:

Swift
```swift
  let numbers = [1, 2, 3, 4, 5, 6, 7, 8, 9, 10]

  // Filtering
  let evenNumbers = numbers.filter { $0 % 2 == 0 }
  print("Even numbers: \(evenNumbers)")

  // Mapping
  let squaredNumbers = numbers.map { $0 * $0 }
  print("Squared numbers: \(squaredNumbers)")

  // Sorting
  let sortedNumbers = numbers.sorted(by: >)
  print("Sorted numbers: \(sortedNumbers)")
```

Explanation of the Code:

filter()` creates a new array containing only the even numbers.

map()` creates a new array containing the squared values.

sorted(by:)` creates a new array with the numbers sorted in descending order

7.1.6 Best Practices:
Vivid Explanation:

Use array literals to create arrays with initial values.

Use type annotations to create empty arrays.

Use indices to access and modify array elements.

Use `for-in` loops to iterate over arrays.

Use array operations to manipulate arrays efficiently.

Use descriptive variable names to improve readability.

By covering these aspects, you'll provide your readers with a comprehensive understanding of how to work with arrays in Swift.

7.2 Dictionaries: Key-Value Pair Storage

Introduction:

Vivid Explanation:

Dictionaries are unordered collections of key-value pairs. They allow you to store and retrieve values using unique keys. Dictionaries are essential for representing data with associations, such as configuration settings, data models, and lookup tables.

This section will explain how to create, access, modify, and iterate over dictionaries in Swift, covering various aspects such as dictionary initialization, adding and removing key-value pairs, and dictionary operations.

7.2.1 Creating Dictionaries:

Vivid Explanation:

You can create dictionaries in Swift using dictionary literals, initializers, and type annotations.

Think of dictionaries as real-world dictionaries, where each word (key) has a corresponding definition (value).

Code Examples:

Swift
```
// Dictionary literal
let ages = ["Alice": 30, "Bob": 25, "Charlie": 35]

// Empty dictionary with type annotation
var scores: [String: Int] = [:]
```

```
// Dictionary initializer
let emptyDict = Dictionary<String, String>()
```

Explanation of the Code:

The `ages` dictionary is created using a dictionary literal.

The `scores` dictionary is created as an empty dictionary of `String` keys and `Int` values.

The `emptyDict` dictionary is created using the `Dictionary<Key, Value>()` initializer.

7.2.2 Accessing Dictionary Values:
Vivid Explanation:
You can access dictionary values using their keys. Since dictionaries are unordered, you cannot access values by index.

Think of keys as the unique identifiers that allow you to retrieve specific values.

Code Examples:
Swift

```
    let capitals = ["USA": "Washington D.C.", "France": "Paris",
"Japan": "Tokyo"]

    let usaCapital = capitals["USA"] // Accesses the value for the
key "USA"
    let franceCapital = capitals["France"] // Accesses the value for
the key "France"

    print("USA Capital: \(usaCapital)")
    print("France Capital: \(franceCapital)")
```

Explanation of the Code:

capitals["USA"]` accesses the value associated with the key "USA".

capitals["France"]` accesses the value associated with the key "France".

Because accessing a key that does not exist returns an optional, it is important to unwrap the value.

7.2.3 Modifying Dictionaries:
Vivid Explanation:

You can modify dictionaries by adding, removing, or changing key-value pairs. Swift provides various methods for these operations.

Modifying dictionaries is like updating the contents of a real-world dictionary, adding, removing, or changing definitions.

Code Examples:

Swift
```
var fruits = ["apple": 3, "banana": 5]

// Adding key-value pairs
fruits["orange"] = 7
fruits.updateValue(10, forKey: "grape")

// Changing values
fruits["apple"] = 4

// Removing key-value pairs
fruits.removeValue(forKey: "banana")
```

```
fruits["grape"] = nil

print("Fruits: \(fruits)")
```

Explanation of the Code:

fruits["orange"] = 7` adds a new key-value pair.

updateValue(forKey:)` adds or updates a value for a key.

fruits["apple"] = 4` changes the value for the key "apple".

removeValue(forKey:)` removes a key-value pair.

Setting a dictionaries key to nil, will also remove that key and value

7.2.4 Iterating Over Dictionaries:

Vivid Explanation:

You can iterate over dictionaries using `for-in` loops, allowing you to process each key-value pair in the dictionary.

Iterating over dictionaries is like going through each word and definition in a real-world dictionary.

Code Examples:
Swift
```
let students = ["Alice": 90, "Bob": 85, "Charlie": 95]

for (name, score) in students {
    print("\(name)'s score: \(score)")
}

for name in students.keys{
```

```swift
    print("Student name: \(name)")
}

for score in students.values{
    print("Student score: \(score)")
}
```

Explanation of the Code:

The `for-in` loop iterates over each key-value pair in the `students` dictionary.

The for-in loop can also iterate over just the keys, or just the values.

7.2.5 Dictionary Operations:
Vivid Explanation:

Swift provides various dictionary operations, such as filtering and mapping, which allow you to manipulate dictionaries efficiently.

Dictionary operations are like tools for transforming and manipulating key-value pairs.

Code Examples:
Swift
```swift
let numbers = ["one": 1, "two": 2, "three": 3, "four": 4, "five": 5]

// Filtering
let evenNumbers = numbers.filter { $0.value % 2 == 0 }
print("Even numbers: \(evenNumbers)")

// Mapping
let squaredNumbers = numbers.mapValues { $0 * $0 }
print("Squared numbers: \(squaredNumbers)")
```

Explanation of the Code:

filter()` creates a new dictionary containing only the key-value pairs with even values.

mapValues()` creates a new dictionary containing the squared values.

7.2.6 Best Practices:
Vivid Explanation:

Use dictionary literals to create dictionaries with initial key-value pairs.

Use type annotations to create empty dictionaries.

Use keys to access and modify dictionary values.

Use for-in loops to iterate over dictionaries.

Use dictionary operations to manipulate dictionaries efficiently.

Use descriptive variable names to improve readability.

7.3 Sets: Unordered Collections of Unique Values

Introduction:

Vivid Explanation:

Sets are unordered collections of unique values of the same type. They are used when you need to store a collection of items without duplicates and when the order of the items doesn't matter. Sets are efficient for checking membership and performing set operations like union, intersection, and difference.

This section will explain how to create, access, modify, and perform operations on sets in Swift, covering various aspects such as set initialization, adding and removing elements, and set operations.

7.3.1 Creating Sets:

Vivid Explanation:

You can create sets in Swift using set literals, initializers, and type annotations.

Think of sets as bags of unique items, where each item appears only once, and the order of items is irrelevant.

Code Examples:

Swift
```
// Set literal
let uniqueNumbers: Set<Int> = [1, 2, 3, 4, 5]
```

```swift
// Empty set with type annotation
var uniqueNames: Set<String> = []

// Set initializer
let emptySet = Set<Double>()
```

Explanation of the Code:

The `uniqueNumbers` set is created using a set literal.

The `uniqueNames` set is created as an empty set of strings.

The `emptySet` set is created using the `Set<Element>()` initializer.

7.3.2 Accessing Set Elements:
Vivid Explanation:

Since sets are unordered, you cannot access elements by index. However, you can check if a set contains a specific element using the `contains()` method.

Think of checking membership as asking if a specific item is present in the bag of unique items.

Code Examples:
Swift
```swift
let colors: Set<String> = ["red", "green", "blue"]

let containsRed = colors.contains("red") // Checks if the set contains "red"
let containsYellow = colors.contains("yellow") // Checks if the set contains "yellow"

print("Contains red: \(containsRed)")
```

```
print("Contains yellow: \(containsYellow)")
```

Explanation of the Code:

colors.contains("red")` checks if the `colors` set contains the element "red".

colors.contains("yellow")` checks if the `colors` set contains the element "yellow".

7.3.3 Modifying Sets:
Vivid Explanation:

You can modify sets by adding or removing elements. Swift provides various methods for these operations.

Modifying sets is like adding or removing unique items from the bag.

Code Examples:
Swift

```
var numbers: Set<Int> = [1, 2, 3]

// Adding elements
numbers.insert(4)
numbers.insert(3) // Inserting an existing element has no effect

// Removing elements
numbers.remove(2)
numbers.remove(5) // Removing a non-existent element has no effect

print("Numbers: \(numbers)")
```

Explanation of the Code:

`numbers.insert(4)` adds the element 4 to the `numbers` set.

numbers.insert(3)` has no effect because 3 is already in the set.

numbers.remove(2)` removes the element 2 from the `numbers` set.

numbers.remove(5)` has no effect because 5 is not in the set.

7.3.4 Iterating Over Sets:
Vivid Explanation:

You can iterate over sets using `for-in` loops, allowing you to process each element in the set. However, the order of iteration is not guaranteed.

Iterating over sets is like going through each unique item in the bag, without a specific order.

Code Examples:

Swift
```
let letters: Set<Character> = ["a", "b", "c"]

for letter in letters {
    print("Letter: \(letter)")
}
```

Explanation of the Code:

The `for-in` loop iterates over each element in the `letters` set.

7.3.5 Set Operations:
Vivid Explanation:
Swift provides various set operations, such as union, intersection, difference, and symmetric difference, which allow you to manipulate sets efficiently.

Set operations are like combining, intersecting, and subtracting bags of unique items.

Code Examples:
Swift
```
let setA: Set<Int> = [1, 2, 3, 4]
let setB: Set<Int> = [3, 4, 5, 6]

// Union
let unionSet = setA.union(setB)
print("Union: \(unionSet)")

// Intersection
let intersectionSet = setA.intersection(setB)
print("Intersection: \(intersectionSet)")

// Difference
let differenceSet = setA.subtracting(setB)
print("Difference: \(differenceSet)")

// Symmetric difference
let symmetricDifferenceSet = setA.symmetricDifference(setB)
print("Symmetric difference: \(symmetricDifferenceSet)")
```

Explanation of the Code:

union()` combines the elements of both sets.

intersection()` finds the common elements between the sets.

subtracting()` finds the elements in setA that are not in setB.

symmetricDifference()` finds the elements that are in either setA or setB, but not in both

7.3.6 Best Practices:

Vivid Explanation:

Use set literals to create sets with initial values.

Use type annotations to create empty sets.

Use `contains()` to check for membership.

Use `for-in` loops to iterate over sets.

Use set operations to manipulate sets efficiently.

Use descriptive variable names to improve readability.

Chapter 8

SwiftUI Fundamentals

8.1 Introduction to SwiftUI: Declarative UI

Introduction:

Vivid Explanation:

SwiftUI is Apple's modern framework for building user interfaces (UIs) across all Apple platforms. It introduces a declarative approach to UI development, allowing you to describe what your UI should look like rather than how to create it. This simplifies UI development, making it more intuitive and efficient.

This section will provide an introduction to SwiftUI, explaining its declarative nature, key concepts, and how it differs from traditional imperative UI frameworks

8.1.1 What is Declarative UI?

Vivid Explanation:

Declarative UI means that you describe the desired state of your UI, and the system takes care of the details of how to render it. You specify what your UI should look like, and SwiftUI automatically updates the UI when the underlying data changes.

Think of declarative UI as telling a painter what you want the painting to look like, rather than telling them each brush stroke to make.

Key Differences from Imperative UI:

Imperative UI: You write code to explicitly create and manipulate UI elements. You manage the state and update the UI manually.

Declarative UI: You describe the desired state of the UI, and the framework automatically updates the UI when the state changes.

Example:

Imperative: "Create a button, set its title, add it to the view, and update its title when the user taps it."

Declarative: "Create a button with a title, and update the title when the data changes."

8.1.2 Key Concepts in SwiftUI:

Vivid Explanation:

SwiftUI introduces several key concepts that are essential for building UIs:

Views: Basic building blocks of SwiftUI UIs. They are lightweight, composable structs that represent UI elements.

Modifiers: Functions that modify the appearance or behavior of views.

State: Data that can change and cause the UI to update.

Layout: SwiftUI automatically manages the layout of views, making it easier to create responsive UIs.

Previews: Xcode provides live previews of your SwiftUI code, allowing you to see changes in real-time.

Code Examples:

Swift

```swift
import SwiftUI

struct ContentView: View {
    @State private var message = "Hello, SwiftUI!"

    var body: some View {
        VStack {
            Text(message)
                .font(.title)
                .padding()

            Button("Change Message") {
                message = "Message Changed!"
            }
            .padding()
        }
    }
}

struct ContentView_Previews: PreviewProvider {
    static var previews: some View {
        ContentView()
    }
}
```

Explanation of the Code:

ContentView` is a `View` struct that defines the UI.

@State` property wrapper declares a state variable `message`.

VStack` is a layout container that arranges views vertically.

Text` and `Button` are basic UI elements.

font(.title)` and `padding()` are modifiers.

ContentView_Previews` provides a live preview of the UI.

8.1.3 Benefits of SwiftUI:
Vivid Explanation:

SwiftUI offers several benefits over traditional imperative UI frameworks

Concise Code: Declarative syntax reduces the amount of code you need to write.

Cross-Platform Compatibility: SwiftUI allows you to build UIs for all Apple platforms with a single codebase.

Live Previews: Xcode's live previews provide instant feedback, making development faster and more efficient.

Automatic UI Updates: SwiftUI automatically updates the UI when the state changes, reducing the risk of bugs.

Easy Layout: SwiftUI's layout system simplifies the creation of responsive UIs

8.1.4 Getting Started with SwiftUI:

Vivid Explanation:

To get started with SwiftUI, you need Xcode 11 or later. You can create a new SwiftUI project in Xcode by selecting "File" -> "New"

-> "Project..." and choosing the "App" template with SwiftUI as the interface.

Xcode previews are very useful, enable them in the canvas window.

8.1.5 Best Practices:

Vivid Explanation
Embrace the declarative approach and focus on describing the desired state of your UI.

Use `@State` to manage data that can change and cause the UI to update.

Use modifiers to customize the appearance and behavior of views.

Use layout containers to organize your UI.

Use live previews to iterate quickly and see changes in real-time.

Break down complex UIs into smaller, reusable views.

8.2 Building Basic UI Elements: Text, Images, and Buttons

Introduction:

Vivid Explanation:

SwiftUI provides a rich set of built-in views for creating user interfaces. Among the most fundamental are Text, Image, and Button. These elements allow you to display text, images, and create interactive elements in your app.

This section will explain how to use these basic UI elements, covering various aspects such as customization, layout, and interaction.

8.2.1 Text:

Vivid Explanation:

The Text view is used to display text in your SwiftUI interface. You can customize the font, color, alignment, and other properties of the text.

Think of Text as a label or a paragraph that displays textual information.

Code Examples:
Swift
```
import SwiftUI

struct TextView: View {
```

```swift
    var body: some View {
      VStack {
        Text("Hello, SwiftUI!")
            .font(.title)
            .foregroundColor(.blue)
            .padding()

            Text("This is a multiline text example.\nIt spans across
multiple lines.")
              .multilineTextAlignment(.center)
              .padding()
      }
    }
  }

  struct TextView_Previews: PreviewProvider {
    static var previews: some View {
      TextView()
    }
  }
```

Explanation of the Code:

The first `Text` view displays "Hello, SwiftUI!" with a title font and blue color.

The second `Text` view displays a multiline text with center alignment.

font()` and `.foregroundColor()` are modifiers that customize the text's appearance.

multilineTextAlignment()` sets the alignment for multiline text

8.2.2 Image:
Vivid Explanation:

The `Image` view is used to display images in your SwiftUI interface. You can display images from your assets catalog or from system symbols.

Think of `Image` as a picture frame that displays visual content.

Code Examples:

Swift

```
import SwiftUI

struct ImageView: View {
    var body: some View {
        VStack {
            Image("swift-logo") // Image from assets catalog
                .resizable()
                .scaledToFit()
                .frame(width: 200, height: 200)
                .padding()

            Image(systemName: "star.fill") // System symbol
                .font(.system(size: 50))
                .foregroundColor(.yellow)
        }
    }
}

struct ImageView_Previews: PreviewProvider {
    static var previews: some View {
        ImageView()
    }
}
```

Explanation of the Code:

The first `Image` view displays an image named "swift-logo" from the assets catalog.

resizable()` allows the image to be resized.

.scaledToFit()` scales the image to fit within the frame.

frame()` sets the size of the image.

The second `Image` view displays a system symbol "star.fill" with a yellow color.

8.2.3 Button:
Vivid Explanation:

The `Button` view is used to create interactive buttons in your SwiftUI interface. You can customize the button's appearance and define an action to be performed when the button is tapped.

Think of `Button` as a clickable element that triggers an action.

Code Examples:
Swift

```
import SwiftUI

struct ButtonView: View {
    @State private var buttonTapped = false

    var body: some View {
        VStack {
            Button(action: {
                buttonTapped.toggle()
```

```
            }) {
                Text(buttonTapped ? "Button Tapped!" : "Tap Me")
                    .padding()
                            .background(buttonTapped ? Color.green :
Color.blue)
                    .foregroundColor(.white)
                    .cornerRadius(10)
            }

            Text(buttonTapped ? "Button was tapped" : "Button was
not tapped")
        }
    }
}

struct ButtonView_Previews: PreviewProvider {
    static var previews: some View {
        ButtonView()
    }
}
```

Explanation of the Code:

The `Button` view has an action that toggles the `buttonTapped` state.

The button's text, background color, and corner radius change based on the `buttonTapped` state.

The second Text view displays the current state of buttonTapped.

8.2.4 Customization and Layout:
Vivid Explanation:

You can customize the appearance and layout of these basic UI elements using modifiers. You can also use layout containers like VStack, HStack, and ZStack to arrange views.

Customization and layout allow you to create visually appealing and well-organized UIs.
Key Modifiers:

.font(): Sets the font of the text.

.foregroundColor(): Sets the color of the text or image.

.padding(): Adds padding around the view.

.frame(): Sets the size and alignment of the view.

.background(): Sets the background color or view.

.cornerRadius(): Sets the corner radius of the view.

8.2.5 Best Practices:
Vivid Explanation:

Use Text views to display clear and concise text.

Use Image views to display high-quality images.

Use Button views to create interactive elements with clear actions

Use modifiers to customize the appearance and layout of views.

Use layout containers to organize your UI.

Use previews to iterate quickly and see changes in real-time.

By covering these aspects, you'll provide your readers with a comprehensive understanding of how to build basic UI elements in SwiftUI.

8.3 Layout and Navigation in SwiftUI

Introduction:

Vivid Explanation:

Layout and navigation are essential aspects of building user interfaces. SwiftUI provides powerful tools for arranging views and creating seamless navigation experiences. With layout containers and navigation views, you can create responsive and user-friendly apps.

This section will explain how to use layout containers and navigation views in SwiftUI, covering various aspects such as VStack, HStack, ZStack, NavigationView, and NavigationLink.

8.3.1 Layout Containers:

Vivid Explanation:

Layout containers are views that arrange their child views in a specific way. SwiftUI provides three primary layout containers: VStack (vertical stack), HStack (horizontal stack), and ZStack (z-index stack).

Think of layout containers as organizers that arrange your UI elements in a structured manner.

Code Examples:

Swift

```swift
import SwiftUI

struct LayoutView: View {
    var body: some View {
        VStack {
            Text("Vertical Stack")
                .font(.title)

            HStack {
                Text("Horizontal")
                Text("Stack")
            }

            ZStack {
                Rectangle()
                    .fill(Color.blue)
                    .frame(width: 200, height: 100)

                Text("Z-Index Stack")
                    .foregroundColor(.white)
            }
        }
        .padding()
    }
}

struct LayoutView_Previews: PreviewProvider {
    static var previews: some View {
        LayoutView()
    }
}
```

Explanation of the Code:

VStack` arranges the `Text` views vertically.

HStack` arranges the `Text` views horizontally.

ZStack` overlays the `Text` view on top of the `Rectangle` view.

8.3.2 NavigationView and NavigationLink:

Vivid Explanation:

NavigationView is a container view that manages navigation between different views. NavigationLink is used to create a tappable element that navigates to another view.

Think of NavigationView as a navigation bar and NavigationLink as a button that takes you to another screen.

Code Examples:

Swift

```
import SwiftUI

struct MainView: View {
    var body: some View {
        NavigationView {
            VStack {
                Text("Main View")
                    .font(.title)
                    .padding()

                NavigationLink(destination: DetailView()) {
                    Text("Go to Detail View")
                        .padding()
                        .background(Color.blue)
                        .foregroundColor(.white)
```

```
                    .cornerRadius(10)
                }
            }
            .navigationTitle("Navigation Example")
        }
    }
}

struct DetailView: View {
    var body: some View {
        Text("Detail View")
            .font(.title)
            .navigationTitle("Detail")
    }
}

struct MainView_Previews: PreviewProvider {
    static var previews: some View {
        MainView()
    }
}
```

Explanation of the Code:

NavigationView` wraps the `VStack` and manages the navigation.

NavigationLink` navigates to `DetailView` when tapped.

navigationTitle()` sets the title of the navigation bar.

8.3.3 Modifiers for Layout and Navigation:
Vivid Explanation:

SwiftUI provides various modifiers to customize the layout and navigation of views.

Modifiers allow you to fine-tune the appearance and behavior of your UI elements
Key Modifiers:

`.padding()`: Adds padding around the view.

`.frame()`: Sets the size and alignment of the view.

`.background()`: Sets the background color or view.

`.cornerRadius()`: Sets the corner radius of the view.

`.navigationTitle()`: Sets the title of the navigation bar.

`.navigationBarItems()`: Adds buttons or other views to the navigation bar.

8.3.4 Best Practices for Layout:
Vivid Explanation:

Use layout containers to organize your UI elements effectively.

Use modifiers to customize the appearance and behavior of views.

Use previews to iterate quickly and see changes in real-time.

Break down complex layouts into smaller, reusable views.

Use `.padding()` and `.frame()` to control the spacing and size of views.

Use `.alignment` property to control the alignment of views within layout containers.

8.3.5 Best Practices for Navigation:

Vivid Explanation:

Use `NavigationView` to manage navigation between different views.

Use `NavigationLink` to create tappable elements that navigate to other views.

Use `.navigationTitle()` to set the title of the navigation bar.

Use `.navigationBarItems()` to add buttons or other views to the navigation bar.

Keep navigation consistent and intuitive for users.

Use descriptive titles for navigation bars and links.

Chapter 9

Advanced Swift Concepts

9.1 Generics: Writing Reusable Code

Introduction:

Vivid Explanation:

Generics are one of the most powerful features in Swift, allowing you to write flexible and reusable code that can work with any type. They enable you to define functions, structures, and classes that are type-agnostic, reducing code duplication and improving code maintainability.

This section will explain what generics are, how to define and use generic functions, structures, and classes, and the benefits of using generics in Swift.

9.1.1 What Are Generics?

Vivid Explanation:

Generics allow you to write code that works with any type, without specifying the exact type until the code is used. They introduce type parameters, which act as placeholders for actual types.

Think of generics as templates or blueprints that can be used to create code that works with different types.

Benefits of Generics:

Code Reusability: Write code once and use it with different types.

Type Safety: Ensure that the code works correctly with the specified types.

Performance: Avoid the overhead of type casting and boxing/unboxing.

9.1.2 Generic Functions:

Vivid Explanation:

Generic functions are functions that can work with any type. They use type parameters to specify the types of their parameters and return values.

Think of generic functions as versatile tools that can handle different types of data.

Code Examples:

Swift

```swift
func swapTwoValues<T>(_ a: inout T, _ b: inout T) {
    let temporaryA = a
    a = b
    b = temporaryA
}

var intA = 10
var intB = 20
swapTwoValues(&intA, &intB)
print("intA: \(intA), intB: \(intB)") // Output: intA: 20, intB: 10
```

```
var stringA = "Hello"
var stringB = "World"
swapTwoValues(&stringA, &stringB)
  print("stringA: \(stringA), stringB: \(stringB)") // Output: stringA:
World, stringB: Hello
```

Explanation of the Code:

The `swapTwoValues(_:_:)` function is a generic function that can swap two values of any type.

The type parameter `T` is used to specify the type of the parameters.

The function works with both integers and strings.

9.1.3 Generic Structures:
Vivid Explanation:
Generic structures are structures that can work with any type. They use type parameters to specify the types of their properties.

Think of generic structures as flexible containers that can hold different types of data.

Code Examples:
Swift
```
struct Stack<Element> {
    var items: [Element] = []

    mutating func push(_ item: Element) {
        items.append(item)
    }

    mutating func pop() -> Element? {
        return items.popLast()
```

```
    }
}
```

```
var intStack = Stack<Int>()
intStack.push(1)
intStack.push(2)
print("Int Stack: \(intStack.items)") // Output: Int Stack: [1, 2]
```

```
var stringStack = Stack<String>()
stringStack.push("Hello")
stringStack.push("World")
 print("String Stack: \(stringStack.items)") // Output: String Stack:
["Hello", "World"]
```

Explanation of the Code:

The `Stack` structure is a generic structure that can hold elements of any type.

The type parameter `Element` is used to specify the type of the items array.

The structure works with both integers and strings.

9.1.4 Generic Classes:
Vivid Explanation:

Generic classes are classes that can work with any type. They use type parameters to specify the types of their properties and methods.

Think of generic classes as adaptable blueprints that can create objects of different types.

Code Examples:

Swift

```swift
class GenericData<T> {
    var data: T

    init(data: T) {
        self.data = data
    }

    func getData() -> T {
        return data
    }
}

let intData = GenericData<Int>(data: 42)
print("Int Data: \(intData.getData())") // Output: Int Data: 42

let stringData = GenericData<String>(data: "Swift")
    print("String Data: \(stringData.getData())") // Output: String
Data: Swift
```

Explanation of the Code:

The `GenericData` class is a generic class that can hold data of any type.

The type parameter `T` is used to specify the type of the data property.

The class works with both integers and strings.

9.1.5 Type Constraints:
Vivid Explanation:

Type constraints allow you to specify requirements for the types that can be used with generic functions, structures, and classes. They ensure that the generic code works correctly with the specified types.

Think of type constraints as rules that specify which types can be used with the generic code.

Code Examples:
Swift
```
   func findIndex<T: Equatable>(of valueToFind: T, in array: [T]) ->
Int? {
      for (index, value) in array.enumerated() {
         if value == valueToFind {
            return index
         }
      }
      return nil
   }

   let numbers = [1, 2, 3, 4, 5]
   let index = findIndex(of: 3, in: numbers)
   print("Index of 3: \(index)") // Output: Index of 3: Optional(2)
```

Explanation of the Code:

The `findIndex(of:in:)` function is a generic function that can find the index of a value in an array.

The type constraint `T: Equatable` specifies that the type `T` must conform to the `Equatable` protocol.

9.1.6 Best Practices:
Vivid Explanation:

Use generics to write reusable code that can work with any type.

Use type parameters to specify the types of parameters, properties, and return values.

Use type constraints to specify requirements for the types that can be used with generic code.

Use descriptive type parameter names to improve readability.

Use generics to reduce code duplication and improve code maintainability

9.2 Protocols and Extensions: Adding Functionality

Introduction:

Vivid Explanation:

Protocols and extensions are powerful features in Swift that allow you to add functionality to existing types. Protocols define a blueprint of methods, properties, and other requirements that suit a particular task or piece of functionality.[1] Extensions allow you to add new functionality to existing types without modifying their original source code.

This section will explain what protocols and extensions are, how to define and use them, and the benefits of using protocols and extensions in Swift.

9.2.1 Protocols:
Vivid Explanation:

Protocols define a blueprint of methods, properties, and other requirements that suit a particular task or piece of functionality.[2] Types that conform to a protocol must implement these requirements.

Think of protocols as contracts that specify what a type must do or provide.

Code Examples:
Swift

```
protocol Printable {
    var description: String { get }
    func printDescription()
}

struct Point: Printable {
    var x: Int
    var y: Int

    var description: String {
        return "Point(x: \(x), y: \(y))"
    }

    func printDescription() {
        print(description)
    }
}

let myPoint = Point(x: 10, y: 20)
myPoint.printDescription() // Output: Point(x: 10, y: 20)
```

Explanation of the Code:

The `Printable` protocol defines a `description` property and a `printDescription()` method.

The `Point` struct conforms to the `Printable` protocol and implements the required property and method.

9.2.2 Protocol Inheritance:
Vivid Explanation:

Protocols can inherit from other protocols, allowing you to create more specialized protocols that build upon existing ones.

Think of protocol inheritance as creating a more specific contract based on a general contract.

Code Examples:
Swift

```
protocol Named {
    var name: String { get }
}

protocol FullNamed: Named {
    var fullName: String { get }
}

struct Person: FullNamed {
    var name: String
    var fullName: String
}

let person = Person(name: "Alice", fullName: "Alice Smith")
print(person.name) // Output: Alice
print(person.fullName) // Output: Alice Smith
```

Explanation of the Code:

The `FullNamed` protocol inherits from the `Named` protocol.

The `Person` struct conforms to the `FullNamed` protocol and must implement both `name` and `fullName` properties

9.2.3 Extensions:
Vivid Explanation:

Extensions allow you to add new functionality to existing types without modifying their original source code. You can add computed properties, methods, initializers, and conform to protocols using extensions.

Think of extensions as adding extra features to a type without changing its core structure

Code Examples:

Swift
```
extension Int {
    var squared: Int {
        return self * self
    }

    func isEven() -> Bool {
        return self % 2 == 0
    }
}

let number = 5
print(number.squared) // Output: 25
print(number.isEven()) // Output: false
```

Explanation of the Code:

The `Int` type is extended with a `squared` computed property and an `isEven()` method

9.2.4 Protocol Extensions:
Vivid Explanation:

Protocol extensions allow you to provide default implementations for protocol requirements. This makes it easier to adopt protocols and provides a form of default behavior.

Think of protocol extensions as providing default actions for a contract

Code Examples:

Swift
```
extension Printable {
    func printDescription() {
        print("Default description: \(description)")
    }
}

struct AnotherPoint: Printable {
    var x: Int
    var y: Int

    var description: String {
        return "AnotherPoint(x: \(x), y: \(y))"
    }
}

let anotherPoint = AnotherPoint(x: 30, y: 40)
```

anotherPoint.printDescription() // Output: Default description: AnotherPoint(x: 30, y: 40)

Explanation of the Code:

The `Printable` protocol is extended with a default implementation for `printDescription()`.

The `AnotherPoint` struct conforms to `Printable` but doesn't need to implement `printDescription()` explicitly.

9.2.5 Benefits of Protocols and Extensions:

Vivid Explanation:

Code Reusability: Protocols allow you to write generic code that can work with any type that conforms to the protocol.

Code Organization: Extensions allow you to organize your code by grouping related functionality

Modularity: Protocols and extensions promote modularity by allowing you to add functionality to existing types without modifying their original source code.

Flexibility: Protocol extensions provide default implementations, making it easier to adopt protocols.

9.2.6 Best Practices:

Vivid Explanation:

Use protocols to define contracts for types.

Use protocol inheritance to create specialized protocols.

Use extensions to add functionality to existing types.

Use protocol extensions to provide default implementations.

Use descriptive names for protocols and extensions.

Keep protocols and extensions focused on specific tasks or functionality.

By covering these aspects, you'll provide your readers with a comprehensive understanding of how to use protocols and extensions in Swift.

9.3 Concurrency and Asynchronous Programming

Introduction:

Concurrency and asynchronous programming are essential for building responsive and efficient applications, especially in today's multi-core and network-dependent world. They allow you to perform multiple tasks simultaneously or handle long-running operations without blocking the main thread, ensuring a smooth user experience.

This section will explain the concepts of concurrency and asynchronous programming in Swift, covering various aspects such as threads, dispatch queues, and the modern `async`/`await` syntax, Actors, and Task groups.

9.3.1 What is Concurrency?

Concurrency is the ability to execute multiple tasks in parallel or in an interleaved manner. It allows your application to make progress on multiple tasks at the same time, improving performance and responsiveness.

Think of concurrency as juggling multiple balls, where you switch between tasks quickly to give the illusion of simultaneous execution.

9.3.2 What is Asynchronous Programming?

Asynchronous programming is a form of concurrency where tasks are executed independently and do not block the main thread. This is particularly useful for long-running operations, such as network requests or file I/O, which can take time to complete.

Think of asynchronous programming as sending a request and continuing with other tasks while waiting for the response.

9.3.3 Threads and Dispatch Queues:

Historically, Swift used threads and dispatch queues to achieve concurrency. Dispatch queues are a way to manage the execution of tasks concurrently or serially.

Threads are the fundamental units of execution in a computer, while dispatch queues provide a higher-level abstraction for managing threads.

Code Examples (Dispatch Queues):

Swift
```
  import Foundation

  func performBackgroundTask() {
     DispatchQueue.global(qos: .background).async {
```

```swift
        // Perform long-running task here
        print("Background task started")
        Thread.sleep(forTimeInterval: 2) // Simulate a long task
        print("Background task completed")

        DispatchQueue.main.async {
            // Update UI on the main thread
            print("Updating UI on main thread")
        }
    }
}

performBackgroundTask()
```

Explanation of the Code:

DispatchQueue.global(qos: .background).async` executes the task on a background queue.

DispatchQueue.main.async` executes the task on the main queue, which is used for updating the UI

9.3.4 Async/Await Syntax:

Swift introduced the `async/await` syntax to simplify asynchronous programming. It provides a more readable and intuitive way to write asynchronous code, making it easier to manage and understand.

Think of `async/await` as a way to write asynchronous code that looks like synchronous code.

Code Examples (Async/Await):
Swift
```swift
  import Foundation
```

```swift
func fetchData() async throws -> String {
    // Simulate fetching data from a network
        try await Task.sleep(nanoseconds: 2_000_000_000) // 2
seconds
    return "Fetched data"
}

func processData() async {
    do {
        let data = try await fetchData()
        print("Data: \(data)")
    } catch {
        print("Error: \(error)")
    }
}

Task {
    await processData()
}
```

Explanation of the Code:

async` marks a function as asynchronous.

await` suspends the execution of the function until the asynchronous task completes.

try await` handles potential errors during the asynchronous task.

Task { }` creates a new asynchronous task

9.3.5 Actors:

Actors are a new concurrency model in Swift that provide a safe way to access mutable state from multiple concurrent tasks. They prevent data races and ensure that only one task can access an actor's state at a time.

Think of actors as isolated containers that protect their internal state from concurrent access.

Code Examples (Actors):

Swift

```swift
actor Counter {
    var count = 0

    func increment() {
        count += 1
    }

    func getCount() -> Int {
        return count
    }
}

Task {
    let counter = Counter()
    await counter.increment()
    print("Count: \(await counter.getCount())")
}
```

Explanation of the Code:

actor` defines an actor type.

Accessing an actor's properties or methods requires `await`.

9.3.6 Async Let:

Async let, allows for multiple async calls to be made concurrently.

Code Example (Async Let):

Swift

```
import Foundation

func fetchUser(id: Int) async throws -> String {
    try await Task.sleep(nanoseconds: 1_000_000_000)
    return "User \(id)"
}

func fetchPosts(userId: Int) async throws -> [String] {
    try await Task.sleep(nanoseconds: 1_500_000_000)
    return ["Post 1", "Post 2"]
}

func fetchUserData() async {
    do {
        async let user = fetchUser(id: 1)
        async let posts = fetchPosts(userId: 1)

        let fetchedUser = try await user
        let fetchedPosts = try await posts

        print("User: \(fetchedUser)")
        print("Posts: \(fetchedPosts)")
    } catch {
        print("Error: \(error)")
    }
}

Task {
```

```
  await fetchUserData()
}
```

9.3.7 Task Groups:

Task groups allow for dynamic creation of child tasks.

Code Example (Task Groups):
Swift
```
  func sumValues(values: [Int]) async throws -> Int {
    return try await withThrowingTaskGroup(of: Int.self) { group in
      for value in values {
        group.addTask {
          try await Task.sleep(nanoseconds: UInt64.random(in:
1_000_000_000...2_000_000_000))
          return value
        }
      }
      return try await group.reduce(0, +)
    }
  }

  Task {
    do {
      let result = try await sumValues(values: [1, 2, 3, 4, 5])
      print("Sum: \(result)")
    } catch {
      print("Error: \(error)")
    }
  }
```

9.3.8 Best Practices:

Use async/await for modern asynchronous programming.

Use actors to protect mutable state from concurrent access.

Use dispatch queues for background tasks and UI updates.

Avoid blocking the main thread.

Handle errors gracefully in asynchronous code.

Use `Task` to create and manage asynchronous tasks.

Use `async let` for concurrent async calls

Use Task groups for dynamic task creation.

Learn how to cancel tasks.

Understand data races.

Chapter 10

Building Your First iOS App

10.1 Project Setup and App Architecture

Introduction:

Building a solid app starts with a well-organized project setup and a robust architecture. This ensures your code is scalable, testable, and maintainable.

This section will cover how to set up a Swift project, discuss common app architectures, and provide best practices for organizing your codebase.

10.1.1 Project Setup in Xcode:

Vivid Explanation:

Setting up a new project in Xcode involves choosing the appropriate template, configuring project settings, and organizing files.

A well-structured project lays the foundation for efficient development.

Steps:

Create a New Project: Open Xcode, select "File" -> "New" -> "Project...", and choose the appropriate template (e.g., "App" for iOS).

Configure Project Settings: Set the product name, organization identifier, bundle identifier, and other settings.

Organize Files: Create folders for different components (e.g., "Models," "Views," "ViewModels").

Add Assets: Import images, icons, and other assets into the "Assets.xcassets" folder.

Set Deployment Target: Ensure the deployment target matches the minimum supported iOS version.

Key Files:

`AppDelegate.swift` or `App.swift`: Manages the app's lifecycle.

`ContentView.swift`: The initial view of your app (for SwiftUI).

`Assets.xcassets`: Stores app assets.

`Info.plist`: Contains app configuration settings.

10.1.2 Common App Architectures:

Vivid Explanation:

App architecture provides a structural design for your codebase, promoting code reuse and maintainability.

Choosing the right architecture depends on the complexity of your app.

MVC (Model-View-Controller):

Description: Separates the app into three components: Model (data), View (UI), and Controller (logic).

Pros: Simple, widely used.

Cons: Controllers can become massive, leading to code that is hard to maintain.

MVVM (Model-View-ViewModel):

Description: Separates the app into Model, View, and ViewModel (data presentation).

Pros: Improved testability, separation of concerns.

Cons: Can introduce more complexity for simple apps.

VIPER (View-Interactor-Presenter-Entity-Router):

Description: Divides the app into distinct layers with clear responsibilities.

Pros: Highly modular, testable, and maintainable.

Cons: Can be overly complex for small projects.

Clean Architecture:

Description: Focuses on separation of concerns, independency of frameworks and testability.

Pros: Highly testable, maintainable, and flexible.

Cons: Steep learning curve, and can be complex to setup.

SwiftUI and Architecture:

SwiftUI encourages a data-driven approach, often used with MVVM or similar architectures, leveraging `@State`, `@ObservedObject`, and `@EnvironmentObject`.

10.1.3 Organizing Your Codebase:

Vivid Explanation:

A well-organized codebase makes it easier to navigate, understand, and maintain your app.

Consistent naming conventions and clear folder structures are crucial.

Best Practices:

Modularization: Break down your app into smaller, reusable modules.

Folder Structure: Use a consistent folder structure to organize files (e.g., "Models," "Views," "ViewModels," "Services").

Naming Conventions: Follow consistent naming conventions for classes, variables, and methods.

Code Comments: Add clear and concise comments to explain complex logic.

Dependency Management: Use Swift Package Manager or CocoaPods to manage dependencies.

Testing: Write unit tests and UI tests to ensure code quality.

Code Reviews: Conduct regular code reviews to maintain consistency and quality.

Use of extensions: Use extensions to organize code into logical sections.

10.1.4 Dependency Injection:

Vivid Explanation:

Dependency injection is a design pattern that promotes loose coupling between components, making your code more testable and maintainable.

It involves providing dependencies to a class rather than creating them within the class.

Methods:

Constructor Injection: Passing dependencies through the initializer.

Property Injection: Setting dependencies after object creation.

Method Injection: Passing dependencies as method parameters.

10.1.5 Best Practices for Project Setup:

Choose an architecture that aligns with your app's complexity.

Use a consistent folder structure and naming conventions.

Write unit tests and UI tests.

Use dependency injection to promote loose coupling.

Conduct regular code reviews.

Keep dependencies up to date.

Use version control (e.g., Git).

This corrected version ensures the information is accurately placed within chapter 10, subtopic one.

10.2 Connecting UI Elements to Code

Introduction:

Connecting UI elements to code is a fundamental aspect of app development. It allows you to create interactive and dynamic user interfaces by linking visual elements to your application's logic.

This section will cover how to connect UI elements to code using Interface Builder (for UIKit) and SwiftUI, focusing on actions, outlets, and state management.

10.2.1 Connecting UI Elements in UIKit (Interface Builder):

Vivid Explanation:

In UIKit, Interface Builder provides a visual way to design your UI. You can connect UI elements to your code using outlets and actions.

Outlets establish a connection between a UI element and a property in your code, while actions define methods that are called when a UI element is interacted with.

Outlets:

Description: Outlets are used to create a reference to a UI element in your code.

Steps:

Open your storyboard or xib file in Interface Builder.

Control-drag from the UI element to your view controller's code.

Select "Outlet" as the connection type, provide a name, and specify the type.

The outlet will be created as a property in your view controller.

Code Example:

```swift
Swift
  import UIKit

  class ViewController: UIViewController {
      @IBOutlet weak var myLabel: UILabel!

      override func viewDidLoad() {
          super.viewDidLoad()
```

```
        myLabel.text = "Hello, UIKit!"
    }
}
```

Actions:

Description: Actions are used to define methods that are called when a UI element is interacted with (e.g., button tap).

Steps

Open your storyboard or xib file in Interface Builder.

Control-drag from the UI element to your view controller's code.

Select "Action" as the connection type, provide a name, and specify the event.

The action method will be created in your view controller.

Code Example:

Swift

```
import UIKit

class ViewController: UIViewController {
    @IBOutlet weak var myLabel: UILabel!

    @IBAction func buttonTapped(_ sender: UIButton) {
        myLabel.text = "Button Tapped!"
    }
}
```

10.2.2 Connecting UI Elements in SwiftUI:
Vivid Explanation:
In SwiftUI, UI elements are connected to code through state management and event handlers.

SwiftUI's declarative syntax and data binding simplify the process of connecting UI elements to code.

State Management:

Description: `@State` and `@Binding` property wrappers are used to manage the state of UI elements and trigger UI updates.

Code Example:

Swift

```swift
import SwiftUI

struct ContentView: View {
    @State private var message = "Hello, SwiftUI!"

    var body: some View {
        VStack {
            Text(message)
                .padding()

            Button("Change Message") {
                message = "Button Tapped!"
            }
            .padding()
        }
    }
}
```

Event Handlers

Description SwiftUI provides event handlers (e.g., `onTapGesture`, `onChange`) to respond to user interactions.

Code Example:

Swift
```
import SwiftUI

struct ContentView: View {
    @State private var isToggled = false

    var body: some View {
        Toggle("Toggle", isOn: $isToggled)
            .padding()

        Text(isToggled ? "Toggled On" : "Toggled Off")
            .padding()
    }
}
```

10.2.3 Best Practices:

Use Descriptive Names: Use descriptive names for outlets and actions to improve code readability.

Minimize Logic in Views: Keep UI-related logic in view controllers or view models.

Use Data Binding: Leverage data binding to keep UI elements in sync with your data.

Handle Events Properly: Ensure event handlers are implemented correctly to respond to user interactions.

Test UI Interactions: Write UI tests to verify that UI elements are connected to code correctly.

Use `@State` **and** `@Binding` **appropriately:** Understand the difference between these property wrappers and use them correctly in SwiftUI.

Break down complex views: Use subviews and functions to keep your views clean and easy to understand.

10.3 Deploying Your App to the Simulator/Device

Introduction:
Deploying your app to the simulator or a physical device is the final step in the development process. It allows you to test your app in a real-world environment and ensure it functions as expected.

This section will cover how to deploy your app to the simulator and a physical device, focusing on Xcode configurations, signing, and troubleshooting.

10.3.1 Deploying to the Simulator:

Vivid Explanation:

The simulator provides a virtual environment for testing your app on various iOS devices without needing physical hardware.

It's a convenient way to quickly iterate and test your app's functionality.

Steps:

Select a Simulator: In Xcode, choose a simulator from the device selection menu (e.g., "iPhone 14 Pro Max Simulator").

Build and Run: Click the "Run" button (or press Cmd + R) to build and run your app on the selected simulator.

Test: Interact with your app in the simulator to test its features and functionality.

Debug: Use Xcode's debugging tools (breakpoints, console) to identify and fix any issues.

Advantages:

Fast iteration and testing.

No need for physical devices.

Ability to simulate various device configurations.

Limitations:

Some hardware-specific features (e.g., camera, sensors) may not be fully simulated.

Performance may differ from physical devices.

10.3.2 Deploying to a Physical Device:

Vivid Explanation:

Deploying to a physical device provides a more accurate representation of your app's performance and behavior.

It's essential for testing hardware-dependent features and ensuring a smooth user experience.

Steps:

Connect Your Device: Connect your iOS device to your Mac using a USB cable.

Select Your Device: In Xcode, choose your connected device from the device selection menu.

Configure Signing:

Ensure you have an Apple Developer account.

In Xcode, go to your project's target settings, select the "Signing & Capabilities" tab.

Enable "Automatically manage signing" and select your team.

Xcode will create a provisioning profile and signing certificate for your device.

Build and Run: Click the "Run" button (or press Cmd + R) to build and run your app on your device.

Trust the Developer: On your device, go to "Settings" -> "General" -> "VPN & Device Management," and trust the developer profile.

Test: Interact with your app on your device to test its features and functionality.

Debug: Use Xcode's debugging tools (breakpoints, console, device logs) to identify and fix any issues.

Advantages:

Accurate testing of hardware-dependent features.

Real-world performance testing.

Better user experience evaluation.

Limitations:

Requires a physical device and Apple Developer account.

Deployment can be slower compared to the simulator.

10.3.3 Troubleshooting Deployment Issues:

Vivid Explanation:

Deployment issues can arise due to various factors, such as signing problems, device compatibility, or code errors.

Effective troubleshooting is crucial for a smooth deployment process.

Common Issues and Solutions:

Signing Errors:

Ensure your Apple Developer account is active and your signing certificates are valid.

Check your provisioning profile and ensure it includes your device.

Clean the build folder (`Cmd + Shift + K`) and try again.

Device Compatibility:

Verify that your app's deployment target matches your device's iOS version.

Test your app on multiple devices to ensure compatibility.

Code Errors:

Use Xcode's debugging tools to identify and fix code errors.

Check the device logs for error messages.

Connection Issues:

Ensure your device is properly connected to your Mac.

Restart Xcode and your device.

Build Errors:

Clean the build folder.

Check that all of your packages are up to date.

10.3.4 Best Practices:

Test your app on both the simulator and physical devices.

Use Xcode's debugging tools to identify and fix issues.

Keep your Apple Developer account and signing certificates up to date.

Test your app on multiple device configurations.

Regularly clean your build folder.

Keep Xcode and your device's iOS version up to date.

www.ingramcontent.com/pod-product-compliance
Lightning Source LLC
LaVergne TN
LVHW051735050326
832903LV00023B/921